Comfy + Cozy RECIPES

pil
Publications International, Ltd.

Louis Weber, CEO
Publications International, Ltd.
8140 Lehigh Ave
Morton Grove, IL 60053

Pictured on the front cover: Perfect Mac and Cheese *(page 78).*

Pictured on the back cover *(clockwise from top left):* Creamy Tomato Soup *(page 37),* Pull-Apart Garlic Cheese Bread *(page 6),* Double Chocolate Cookies and Cream Mousse *(page 176),* Little Italy Baked Ziti *(page 69),* Biscuit-Topped Steak and Vegetable Pie *(page 148)* and Pulled Chicken Sandwiches *(page 122).*

ISBN: 978-1-63938-996-4

Manufactured in China.

8 7 6 5 4 3 2 1

Microwave Cooking: Microwave ovens vary in wattage. Use the cooking times as guidelines and check for doneness before adding more time.

WARNING: Food preparation, baking and cooking involve inherent dangers: misuse of electric products, sharp electric tools, boiling water, hot stoves, allergic reactions, foodborne illnesses and the like, pose numerous potential risks. Publications International, Ltd. (PIL) assumes no responsibility or liability for any damages you may experience as a result of following recipes, instructions, tips or advice in this publication.

While we hope this publication helps you find new ways to eat delicious foods, you may not always achieve the results desired due to variations in ingredients, cooking temperatures, typos, errors, omissions or individual cooking abilities.

Contents

Bottomless Bread Basket

CHEDDAR BISCUITS

MAKES 15 BISCUITS

- **2 cups all-purpose flour**
- **1 tablespoon sugar**
- **1 tablespoon baking powder**
- **2¼ teaspoons garlic powder, divided**
- **¾ teaspoon plus pinch of salt, divided**
- **1 cup whole milk**
- **½ cup (1 stick) plus 3 tablespoons butter, melted, divided**
- **2 cups (8 ounces) shredded Cheddar cheese**
- **½ teaspoon dried parsley flakes**

1. Preheat oven to 450°F. Line baking sheet with parchment paper.
2. Combine flour, sugar, baking powder, 2 teaspoons garlic powder and ¾ teaspoon salt in large bowl; mix well. Add milk and ½ cup melted butter; stir just until dry ingredients are moistened. Stir in cheese just until blended. Drop scant ¼ cupfuls of dough about 1½ inches apart onto prepared baking sheet.
3. Bake 10 to 12 minutes or until golden brown.
4. Meanwhile, combine remaining 3 tablespoons melted butter, ¼ teaspoon garlic powder, pinch of salt and parsley flakes in small bowl; brush over biscuits immediately after removing from oven. Serve warm.

PULL-APART GARLIC CHEESE BREAD

MAKES 12 SERVINGS

- 3 cups all-purpose flour
- 1 package (¼ ounce) instant yeast
- 1 teaspoon salt
- 1 cup warm water (120°F)
- 2 tablespoons olive oil
- 6 cloves garlic, minced, divided
- ¼ cup (½ stick) butter
- ¼ teaspoon paprika
- 1 cup grated Parmesan cheese
- 1 cup (4 ounces) shredded mozzarella cheese
- ½ cup pizza sauce
- Chopped fresh parsley (optional)

1. Combine flour, yeast and salt in large bowl of stand mixer. Stir in water and oil to form rough dough. Add half of garlic; mix with dough hook at low speed 5 to 7 minutes or until dough is smooth and elastic.
2. Shape dough into a ball. Place in greased bowl; turn to grease top. Cover and let rise in warm place 45 minutes to 1 hour or until doubled in size.
3. Melt butter in small skillet over medium-low heat. Add remaining garlic; cook and stir 1 minute. Stir in paprika; remove from heat. Brush 9-inch springform pan with some of butter mixture. Place 6-ounce ramekin in center of pan. Place Parmesan in shallow bowl.
4. Turn out dough onto lightly floured surface; pat into 9-inch square. Cut into 1-inch squares; roll each square into a ball. Dip half of balls in melted butter mixture; roll in Parmesan to coat. Place around ramekin in prepared pan; sprinkle with ½ cup mozzarella. Repeat with remaining dough balls, butter mixture, Parmesan and mozzarella. Cover and let rise in warm place 1 hour or until dough has risen to top of pan.
5. Preheat oven to 350°F. Line baking sheet with foil. Place springform pan on prepared baking sheet. Pour pizza sauce into ramekin.
6. Bake 20 to 25 minutes or until bread is firm and golden brown. Loosen edges of bread with knife; carefully remove side of pan. Sprinkle with parsley, if desired. Serve warm.

RUSTIC WHITE BREAD

MAKES 1 LOAF

- 5 cups all-purpose flour
- 2 cups warm water (105° to 115°F)
- 1 tablespoon salt
- 1 package (¼ ounce) instant or active dry yeast

1. Combine flour and warm water in large bowl; stir to form shaggy dough. Cover with clean kitchen towel; let stand 30 minutes to hydrate flour.
2. Sprinkle salt and yeast over dough; squeeze and fold with hands to incorporate. Turn out dough onto lightly floured surface; knead 2 minutes, adding additional flour by teaspoonfuls if needed (dough will be sticky). Shape dough into a ball; return to bowl. Cover and let rise 2 hours.
3. Gently fold edges of dough to center, pressing down lightly to form a ball. Turn dough over; cover and let rise 3 to 4 hours or until dough has large air bubbles.
4. Turn oven to 450°F; place 5- to 6-quart Dutch oven with lid in oven. Preheat oven and pot 30 minutes. Meanwhile, gently ease dough from bowl onto work surface with lightly floured hands, trying not to tear dough as much as possible (do not punch down dough). Wrap your hands around sides of dough and gently pull it across work surface to form a ball. Repeat until dough is a smooth ball. Lightly dust medium bowl with flour; place dough in bowl. Cover and let rise while oven and pot are preheating.
5. Use oven mitts to carefully remove Dutch oven from oven and remove lid (pot and lid will be very hot). Gently turn out dough onto work surface; place in Dutch oven, bottom side up. Replace lid using oven mitts; return Dutch oven to oven.
6. Bake bread, covered, 30 minutes. Carefully remove lid; bake 10 to 12 minutes or until top is deep golden brown. Remove to wire rack to cool completely.

SPINACH AND FETA STUFFED CHEESY BREAD

MAKES ABOUT 8 SERVINGS

- 1½ cups (6 ounces) shredded mozzarella or Monterey Jack cheese, divided
- 1 cup (4 ounces) crumbled feta cheese
- ¼ cup plus 1 tablespoon grated Parmesan cheese, divided
- 1 teaspoon minced garlic
- 1 container (11 ounces) refrigerated French bread dough
- 1 cup baby spinach
- ½ cup (2 ounces) shredded Cheddar cheese
- ¼ teaspoon Italian seasoning or dried parsley flakes

1. Preheat oven to 350°F. Line baking sheet with parchment paper.

2. Combine 1 cup mozzarella, feta, ¼ cup Parmesan and garlic in small bowl; mix well. Unroll dough on prepared baking sheet with long side facing you. Spread half of cheese mixture lengthwise over half of dough; top with spinach and remaining half of cheese mixture. Fold dough in half over filling; press long edge gently to seal.

3. Cut crosswise into 1-inch slices (but do not separate slices). Top with Cheddar, then with remaining ½ cup mozzarella. Sprinkle with Italian seasoning.

4. Bake 25 to 30 minutes or until golden brown. Serve warm.

EXTRA CORNY CORN BREAD

MAKES 8 SERVINGS

- **1 cup all-purpose flour**
- **1 cup yellow cornmeal**
- **⅓ cup packed brown sugar**
- **1 teaspoon baking powder**
- **1 teaspoon baking soda**
- **½ teaspoon salt**
- **2 eggs**
- **1 cup buttermilk, at room temperature**
- **½ cup (1 stick) butter, melted and cooled**
- **1 can (about 11 ounces) corn with green and red peppers, drained**

1. Preheat oven to 400°F. Spray 9-inch round cake pan with nonstick cooking spray.*
2. Combine flour, cornmeal, brown sugar, baking powder, baking soda and salt in large bowl; mix well.
3. Beat eggs in medium bowl. Add buttermilk and butter; beat until well blended. Add to flour mixture; stir until blended. Gently stir in corn. Pour batter into prepared pan.
4. Bake 20 to 25 minutes or until top is golden brown and toothpick inserted into center comes out clean. Cool in pan on wire rack 10 minutes. Invert corn bread onto plate; invert again onto cutting board or serving plate.

**Or use 9-inch cast iron skillet; brush with additional melted butter before pouring batter into skillet.*

MONTE CRISTO MONKEY BREAD

MAKES 8 TO 10 SERVINGS

- 2 tablespoons butter, softened
- 2 loaves (16 ounces each) frozen bread dough, thawed according to package directions
- 2 eggs
- ¼ cup whipping cream or milk
- ½ teaspoon salt
- 4 ounces sliced deli turkey, coarsely chopped
- 2 ounces sliced deli ham, coarsely chopped
- 8 ounces Swiss cheese, cut into ¼-inch cubes
- ¼ cup red currant or raspberry jam, plus additional for serving
- Powdered sugar

1. Grease 12-inch bundt pan with butter.
2. Shape dough into about 45 (1½-inch) balls. Beat eggs, cream and salt in medium bowl until blended.
3. Dip nine dough balls into egg mixture; place in prepared pan. Sprinkle with one quarter each of turkey, ham and cheese; drop 1 tablespoon jam by ½ teaspoonfuls over filling. Repeat layers three times; top with remaining dough balls. Cover and let rise in warm place about 30 minutes or until dough is puffy. Preheat oven to 350°F.
4. Bake 40 minutes or until bread is firm and golden brown. Loosen bread from side of pan; invert onto plate. Carefully invert again onto serving plate. Cool slightly; sprinkle with powdered sugar. Serve warm with additional jam.

RICH AND GOOEY CINNAMON BUNS

MAKES 12 BUNS

Dough

- 1 package (¼ ounce) active dry yeast
- 1 cup warm milk (110°F)
- 2 eggs, beaten
- ½ cup granulated sugar
- ¼ cup (½ stick) butter, softened
- 1 teaspoon salt
- 4 to 4¼ cups all-purpose flour

Filling

- 1 cup packed brown sugar
- 3 tablespoons ground cinnamon
- Pinch salt
- 6 tablespoons (¾ stick) butter, softened

Icing

- 1½ cups powdered sugar
- 3 ounces cream cheese, softened
- ¼ cup (½ stick) butter, softened
- ½ teaspoon vanilla
- ⅛ teaspoon salt

1. Dissolve yeast in warm milk in large bowl of stand mixer. Add eggs, granulated sugar, ¼ cup butter and 1 teaspoon salt; beat at medium speed until well blended. Add 4 cups flour; beat at low speed until dough begins to come together. Mix with dough hook at low speed 5 minutes or until dough is smooth, elastic and slightly sticky. Add additional flour, 1 tablespoon at a time, if necessary to prevent sticking.

2. Shape dough into a ball. Place in large greased bowl; turn to grease top. Cover and let rise in warm place 1 hour or until doubled in size. Meanwhile, for filling, combine brown sugar, cinnamon and pinch of salt in small bowl; mix well.

3. Spray 13×9-inch baking pan with nonstick cooking spray. Roll out dough into 18×14-inch rectangle on floured surface. Spread 6 tablespoons butter evenly over dough; top with cinnamon-sugar mixture. Beginning with long side, roll up dough tightly jelly-roll style; pinch seam to seal. Cut log crosswise into 12 slices; place slices cut sides up in prepared pan. Cover and let rise in warm place 30 minutes or until almost doubled in size. Preheat oven to 350°F.

4. Bake 20 to 25 minutes or until golden brown. Meanwhile, for icing, combine powdered sugar, cream cheese, ¼ cup butter, vanilla and ⅛ teaspoon salt in medium bowl; beat with electric mixer at medium speed 2 minutes or until smooth and creamy. Spread icing generously over warm buns.

SUPER SIMPLE CHEESY BISCUIT BREAD

MAKES 12 SERVINGS

- **2 packages (12 ounces each) refrigerated buttermilk biscuits (10 biscuits per package)**
- **2 tablespoons butter, melted**
- **1½ cups (6 ounces) shredded Italian cheese blend**

1. Preheat oven to 350°F. Spray 9×5-inch loaf pan with nonstick cooking spray.
2. Separate biscuits; cut each biscuit into four pieces with scissors. Layer half of biscuit pieces in prepared pan. Drizzle with 1 tablespoon butter; sprinkle with 1 cup cheese. Top with remaining biscuit pieces, 1 tablespoon butter and ½ cup cheese.
3. Bake 25 minutes or until golden brown. Serve warm.

Tip

It's easy to change up the flavors in this simple bread. Try Mexican cheese blend instead of Italian, and add taco seasoning mix and/or hot pepper sauce to the melted butter before drizzling it over the dough. Or, sprinkle ¼ cup chopped ham, salami or crumbled crisp-cooked bacon between the layers of dough.

CHEDDAR TURTLE BREAD ›

MAKES 8 SERVINGS

- 1 round loaf sourdough or Italian bread (about 16 ounces)
- ½ cup (1 stick) butter, melted
- 2 tablespoons Dijon or yellow mustard
- ½ teaspoon salt
- ½ teaspoon chili powder
- ½ teaspoon garlic powder
- 1½ cups (6 ounces) shredded Cheddar cheese

1. Preheat oven to 350°F.
2. Cut bread into 1-inch slices, cutting two-thirds of the way through (but do not cut through bottom of loaf). Turn loaf and cut into 1-inch slices without cutting through bottom to create grid.
3. Combine butter, mustard, salt, chili powder and garlic powder in small bowl; mix well. Brush cut surfaces of bread with butter mixture. Gently separate bread sticks to loosen; sprinkle cheese between bread sticks. Wrap loaf tightly with foil; place on baking sheet.
4. Bake 30 minutes or until bread is toasted and cheese is melted. Unwrap bread; pull sticks apart to serve.

SKILLET SAUSAGE CORN BREAD

MAKES 10 SERVINGS

- 8 ounces bulk pork sausage
- 1 medium onion, diced
- 1 jalapeño pepper, diced
- 1 package (8½ ounces) corn muffin mix
- 1 cup (4 ounces) shredded Cheddar cheese, divided
- ⅓ cup milk
- 1 egg

1. Preheat oven to 350°F. Cook sausage in large ovenproof skillet over medium heat 6 to 8 minutes or until browned, stirring to break up meat. Add onion and jalapeño; cook and stir 5 minutes or until vegetables are softened. Remove mixture to medium bowl.
2. Combine corn muffin mix, ½ cup cheese, milk and egg in separate medium bowl. Pour batter into skillet; top with sausage mixture. Sprinkle with remaining ½ cup cheese.
3. Bake 20 to 25 minutes or until edges are lightly browned. Cut into wedges.

CRANBERRY BRIE BUBBLE BREAD

MAKES 12 SERVINGS

- 3 cups all-purpose flour
- 1 package (¼ ounce) instant yeast
- 1 teaspoon salt
- 1 cup warm water (120°F)
- ¼ cup (½ stick) plus 2 tablespoons butter, melted, divided
- ¾ cup finely chopped pecans or walnuts
- ¼ cup packed brown sugar
- ¼ teaspoon coarse salt
- 1 package (7 ounces) Brie cheese, cut into ¼-inch pieces
- 1 cup whole-berry cranberry sauce

1. Combine flour, yeast and 1 teaspoon salt in large bowl of stand mixer. Stir in warm water and 2 tablespoons butter to form rough dough. Mix with dough hook at low speed 5 to 7 minutes or until dough is smooth and elastic.

2. Shape dough into a ball. Place in greased bowl; turn to grease top. Cover and let rise in warm place about 45 minutes or until doubled in size.

3. Spray 2-quart baking dish or ovenproof bowl with nonstick cooking spray. Combine pecans, brown sugar and coarse salt in shallow bowl; mix well. Place remaining ¼ cup butter in another shallow bowl.

4. Turn out dough onto lightly floured surface; pat and stretch into 9×6-inch rectangle. Cut dough into 1-inch pieces; roll into balls.

5. Dip balls of dough in butter; roll in pecan mixture to coat. Place in prepared baking dish, layering with cheese and spoonfuls of cranberry sauce. Cover and let rise in warm place about 45 minutes or until dough is puffy. Preheat oven to 350°F.

6. Bake 30 minutes or until dough is firm and filling is bubbly. Cool on wire rack 15 to 20 minutes. Serve warm.

PEPPERONI BREAD

MAKES ABOUT 6 SERVINGS

- 1 package (about 14 ounces) refrigerated pizza dough
- 8 slices provolone cheese
- 20 to 30 slices pepperoni (about half of 6-ounce package)
- ½ teaspoon Italian seasoning
- ¾ cup (3 ounces) shredded mozzarella cheese
- ½ cup grated Parmesan cheese
- 1 egg, beaten
- Marinara sauce, heated

1. Preheat oven to 400°F. Unroll dough on sheet of parchment paper with long side facing you. Cut off corners of dough to create oval shape.
2. Arrange half of provolone slices over bottom half of oval, cutting to fit as necessary. Top with pepperoni; sprinkle with ¼ teaspoon Italian seasoning. Top with mozzarella, Parmesan and remaining provolone slices; sprinkle with remaining ¼ teaspoon Italian seasoning.
3. Fold top half of dough over filling to create half moon (calzone) shape; press edges with fork or pinch edges to seal. Transfer calzone on parchment paper to baking sheet; curve slightly into crescent shape. Brush with beaten egg.
4. Bake 16 minutes or until crust is golden brown. Remove to wire rack to cool slightly. Cut crosswise into slices; serve with marinara sauce.

HAM AND SWISS BISCUITS >

MAKES ABOUT 18 BISCUITS

- 2 cups all-purpose flour
- 2 teaspoons baking powder
- ½ teaspoon baking soda
- ¼ teaspoon salt
- ½ cup (1 stick) cold butter, cut into small pieces
- ⅔ cup buttermilk
- ½ cup (2 ounces) shredded Swiss cheese
- 2 ounces ham, finely chopped

1 Preheat oven to 450°F. Line baking sheet with parchment paper or spray with nonstick cooking spray.

2 Combine flour, baking powder, baking soda and salt in medium bowl; mix well. Cut in butter with pastry blender until mixture resembles coarse crumbs. Stir in buttermilk, 1 tablespoon at a time, until slightly sticky dough forms. Stir in cheese and ham.

3 Turn out dough onto lightly floured surface; knead lightly. Roll out dough to ½-inch thickness. Cut out biscuits with 2-inch round cutter. Place on prepared baking sheet.

4 Bake 10 minutes or until browned. Serve warm.

CHEESY GARLIC BREAD

MAKES 8 TO 10 SERVINGS

- 1 loaf Italian bread (about 16 ounces)
- ½ cup (1 stick) butter, softened
- 8 cloves garlic, very thinly sliced
- ¼ cup grated Parmesan cheese
- 2 cups (8 ounces) shredded mozzarella cheese

1 Preheat oven to 425°F. Line baking sheet with foil.

2 Cut bread in half horizontally. Spread cut sides of bread evenly with butter; top with garlic. Sprinkle with Parmesan, then mozzarella. Place bread on prepared baking sheet.

3 Bake 12 minutes or until cheese is melted and golden brown in spots. Cut bread crosswise into slices. Serve warm.

EASY PEASY PIZZA LOAF

MAKES ABOUT 8 SERVINGS

- 1 loaf (16 ounces) frozen bread dough, thawed according to package directions
- ⅓ cup plus 2 tablespoons pizza sauce, divided
- 1 cup (4 ounces) shredded mozzarella cheese
- ½ cup shredded Parmesan cheese
- 1 egg, beaten

1. Preheat oven to 350°F. Line 9×5-inch loaf pan with parchment paper or spray with nonstick cooking spray.
2. Roll out dough into 20×10-inch rectangle on lightly floured surface. Spread ⅓ cup pizza sauce evenly over dough, leaving ½-inch borders. Sprinkle with mozzarella and Parmesan. Starting with long side, roll up dough jelly-roll style; pinch seam to seal. Cut roll in half lengthwise; turn halves cut sides up. Twist halves together, keeping filling facing up as much as possible.
3. Arrange dough in prepared pan, winding twisted dough back and forth in pan. Brush top of dough with egg. Fill in crevices and folds of dough with spoonfuls of remaining pizza sauce.
4. Bake about 40 minutes or until bread is golden brown and cooked through. (Cover loosely with foil if dough browns too quickly.) Cool in pan on wire rack 10 minutes. Serve warm.

CINNAMON COFFEE MONKEY BREAD

MAKES 10 TO 12 SERVINGS

- ½ cup granulated sugar
- 1 tablespoon ground cinnamon
- 1 tablespoon instant coffee granules
- 3 packages (7½ ounces each) refrigerated buttermilk biscuits (10 biscuits per package)
- Cinnamon Coffee Glaze (recipe follows)

1. Preheat oven to 350°F. Spray 12-cup (10-inch) bundt pan with nonstick cooking spray.
2. Combine granulated sugar, cinnamon and coffee granules in small bowl; mix well.
3. Separate biscuits; cut each biscuit into four pieces with scissors. Roll each piece into a ball; roll balls in sugar mixture to coat. Layer in prepared pan.
4. Bake 30 minutes or until golden brown. Cool in pan on wire rack 5 minutes. Loosen edges of bread with knife; invert onto serving plate.
5. Prepare Cinnamon Coffee Glaze; drizzle over bread. Serve warm.

CINNAMON COFFEE GLAZE

- ½ cup (1 stick) butter
- 1 cup packed brown sugar
- 2 tablespoons ground cinnamon
- 1 teaspoon instant coffee granules

Combine butter, brown sugar, cinnamon and coffee granules in small saucepan; cook and stir over medium-low heat about 2 minutes or until brown sugar is dissolved and glaze is smooth.

Warm + Cozy Bowls

CREAMY TOMATO SOUP

MAKES 6 SERVINGS

- **3 tablespoons olive oil, divided**
- **2 tablespoons butter**
- **1 large onion, finely chopped**
- **2 cloves garlic, minced**
- **2 teaspoons sugar**
- **1 teaspoon salt**
- **½ teaspoon dried oregano**
- **2 cans (28 ounces each) peeled Italian plum tomatoes, undrained**
- **4 cups ½-inch focaccia cubes (half of 9-ounce loaf)**
- **½ teaspoon freshly ground black pepper**
- **½ cup whipping cream**

1. Heat 2 tablespoons oil and butter in large saucepan or Dutch oven over medium-high heat. Add onion; cook and stir 5 minutes or until softened. Add garlic, sugar, salt and oregano; cook and stir 30 seconds. Stir in tomatoes with juice; bring to a boil. Reduce heat to medium-low; simmer 45 minutes, stirring occasionally.

2. Meanwhile, prepare croutons. Preheat oven to 350°F. Combine focaccia cubes, remaining 1 tablespoon oil and pepper in large bowl; toss to coat. Spread on large rimmed baking sheet. Bake 10 minutes or until bread cubes are golden brown.

3. Blend soup with immersion blender until smooth. (Or process soup in batches in food processor or blender.) Stir in cream; cook until heated through. Serve soup topped with croutons.

SAUSAGE AND BEAN STEW

MAKES 4 TO 6 SERVINGS

- **2 cups fresh bread crumbs***
- **2 tablespoons olive oil, divided**
- **1 pound uncooked pork sausage, cut into 2-inch pieces**
- **1 leek, cut in half lengthwise and thinly sliced**
- **1 large onion, cut into quarters and cut into ¼-inch slices**
- **1 teaspoon salt, divided**
- **2 cloves garlic, minced**
- **½ teaspoon dried thyme**
- **½ teaspoon ground sage**
- **¼ teaspoon paprika**
- **¼ teaspoon ground allspice**
- **¼ teaspoon black pepper**
- **1 can (28 ounces) diced tomatoes**
- **2 cans (about 15 ounces each) navy or cannellini beans, rinsed and drained**
- **2 tablespoons whole grain mustard**
- **Fresh thyme leaves (optional)**

To make bread crumbs, cut 4 ounces stale baguette or country bread into several pieces; pulse in food processor until coarse crumbs form.

1. Preheat oven to 350°F. Combine bread crumbs and 1 tablespoon oil in medium bowl; mix well.

2. Heat remaining 1 tablespoon oil in large ovenproof skillet over medium-high heat. Add sausage; cook 8 minutes or until browned, stirring occasionally. (Sausage will not be cooked through.) Remove to plate.

3. Add leek, onion and ½ teaspoon salt to skillet; cook 10 minutes or until vegetables are soft and beginning to brown, stirring occasionally. Add garlic; cook and stir 1 minute. Add dried thyme, sage, paprika, allspice and pepper; cook and stir 1 minute. Add tomatoes; cook 5 minutes, stirring occasionally. Stir in beans, mustard and remaining ½ teaspoon salt; bring to a simmer.

4. Return sausage to skillet, pushing down into bean mixture. Sprinkle with bread crumbs.

5. Bake 25 minutes or until bread crumbs are lightly browned and sausage is cooked through. Garnish with fresh thyme.

CHICKEN AND HOMEMADE NOODLE SOUP

MAKES 4 SERVINGS

- ¾ cup all-purpose flour
- 2 teaspoons finely chopped fresh thyme *or* ½ teaspoon dried thyme, divided
- ¼ teaspoon salt
- 1 egg yolk, beaten
- 2 cups plus 3 tablespoons cold water, divided
- 1 pound boneless skinless chicken thighs, cut into ¾-inch pieces
- 5 cups chicken broth
- 1 onion, chopped
- 1 carrot, thinly sliced
- ¾ cup frozen peas
- Chopped fresh Italian parsley

1. Combine flour, 1 teaspoon thyme and salt in medium bowl. Add egg yolk and 3 tablespoons water; stir until well blended. Shape dough into a ball. Place dough on lightly floured surface; flatten slightly. Knead 5 minutes or until dough is smooth and elastic, adding additional flour to prevent sticking, if necessary. Cover with plastic wrap; let stand 15 minutes.

2. Roll out dough to ⅛-inch thickness or thinner on lightly floured surface. If dough is too elastic, let rest several minutes. Let dough rest about 30 minutes to dry slightly. Cut dough into ¼-inch-wide strips; cut strips 1½ to 2 inches long.

3. Combine chicken and remaining 2 cups water in medium saucepan; bring to a boil over high heat. Reduce heat to medium-low; cover and simmer 5 minutes or until chicken is cooked through. Drain chicken; set aside.

4. Combine broth, onion, carrot and remaining 1 teaspoon thyme in large saucepan; bring to a boil over high heat. Add noodles. Reduce heat to medium-low; cook 8 minutes or until noodles are tender. Stir in chicken and peas; cook 2 minutes or until heated through. Sprinkle with parsley.

BROCCOLI CHEESE SOUP

MAKES 4 TO 6 SERVINGS

- 6 tablespoons (¾ stick) butter
- 1 cup chopped onion
- 1 clove garlic, minced
- ¼ cup all-purpose flour
- 2 cups vegetable broth
- 2 cups milk
- 1½ teaspoons Dijon mustard
- ½ teaspoon salt
- ¼ teaspoon ground nutmeg
- ¼ teaspoon black pepper
- ⅛ teaspoon hot pepper sauce
- 1 package (16 ounces) frozen broccoli (5 cups)
- 2 carrots, shredded (1 cup)
- 6 ounces pasteurized process cheese product, cubed
- 1 cup (4 ounces) shredded sharp Cheddar cheese, plus additional for garnish

1. Melt butter in large saucepan or Dutch oven over medium-low heat. Add onion; cook and stir 8 minutes or until softened. Add garlic; cook and stir 1 minute. Increase heat to medium. Whisk in flour until smooth; cook and stir 3 minutes without browning.

2. Gradually whisk in broth and milk. Add mustard, salt, nutmeg, black pepper and hot pepper sauce; cook 15 minutes or until thickened, stirring occasionally.

3. Add broccoli; cook 15 minutes. Add carrots; cook 10 minutes or until vegetables are tender.

4. Remove half of soup to food processor or blender; process until smooth. Return to saucepan. Add cheese product and 1 cup Cheddar; cook and stir over low heat until cheese is melted. Garnish soup with additional Cheddar.

SOUTHWESTERN CHICKEN CHILI

MAKES 6 SERVINGS

- 1 tablespoon vegetable oil
- 1 small onion, chopped
- 1 small red bell pepper, diced (¼-inch pieces)
- 1 jalapeño pepper, finely chopped
- 6 cloves garlic, minced
- 3 tablespoons all-purpose flour
- 2 tablespoons chili powder
- 1 tablespoon ground cumin
- 2 teaspoons salt
- 1 can (about 15 ounces) kidney beans, rinsed and drained
- 1 can (about 14 ounces) chicken broth
- 1 can (8 ounces) tomato sauce
- 1 can (4 ounces) diced green chiles
- 2 tablespoons chopped fresh cilantro
- 3 cups shredded cooked chicken
- Optional toppings: shredded Cheddar cheese, chopped red onion, blue corn tortilla chips

1. Heat oil in large saucepan over medium heat. Add onion; cook about 5 minutes or until translucent, stirring occasionally. Add bell pepper, jalapeño and garlic; cook and stir 3 minutes. Add flour, chili powder, cumin and salt; cook and stir 1 minute or until spices are fragrant.

2. Stir in beans, broth, tomato sauce, chiles and cilantro; bring to a boil. Reduce heat to low; cover and simmer 20 minutes, stirring occasionally.

3. Stir in chicken; cover and simmer 20 minutes. If chili is too thin, cook, uncovered, until slightly thickened. Serve with desired toppings.

ITALIAN WEDDING SOUP

MAKES 8 SERVINGS

Meatballs

- 2 eggs
- 2 cloves garlic, minced
- 1 teaspoon salt
- ⅛ teaspoon black pepper
- 1½ pounds meat loaf mix (ground beef and pork)
- ¾ cup plain dry bread crumbs
- ½ cup grated Parmesan cheese
- 2 tablespoons olive oil

Soup

- 1 onion, chopped
- 2 carrots, chopped
- 4 cloves garlic, minced
- 2 heads escarole or curly endive, coarsely chopped
- 8 cups chicken broth
- 1 can (about 14 ounces) Italian plum tomatoes, undrained, coarsely chopped
- 3 sprigs fresh thyme
- 1 teaspoon salt
- ½ teaspoon red pepper flakes
- 1 cup uncooked acini di pepe pasta

1. For meatballs, beat eggs, 2 cloves garlic, 1 teaspoon salt and black pepper in large bowl until blended. Stir in meat loaf mix, bread crumbs and cheese; mix gently until well blended. Shape mixture by tablespoonfuls into 1-inch balls.

2. Heat oil in large saucepan or Dutch oven over medium heat. Cook meatballs in batches 5 minutes or until browned. Remove to plate; set aside.

3. For soup, add onion, carrots and 4 cloves garlic to same saucepan; cook and stir 5 minutes or until onion is lightly browned. Add escarole; cook and stir 2 minutes or until wilted. Stir in broth, tomatoes with juice, thyme, 1 teaspoon salt and red pepper flakes; bring to a boil over high heat. Reduce heat to medium-low; simmer 15 minutes.

4. Add meatballs and pasta to soup; return to a boil over high heat. Reduce heat to medium; cook 10 minutes or until pasta is tender. Remove and discard thyme sprigs before serving.

BAKED POTATO SOUP

MAKES 6 TO 8 SERVINGS

- 3 medium russet potatoes (about 1 pound)
- ¼ cup (½ stick) butter
- 1 cup chopped onion
- ½ cup all-purpose flour
- 4 cups chicken or vegetable broth
- 1½ cups instant mashed potato flakes
- 1 cup water
- 1 cup half-and-half
- 1 teaspoon salt
- ½ teaspoon dried basil
- ½ teaspoon dried thyme
- ¼ teaspoon black pepper
- 1 cup (4 ounces) shredded Cheddar cheese
- 4 slices bacon, crisp-cooked and crumbled
- 1 green onion, chopped

1. Preheat oven to 400°F. Scrub potatoes and prick in several places with fork. Place in baking pan; bake 1 hour. Cool completely; peel and cut into ½-inch cubes. (Potatoes can be prepared several days in advance; refrigerate until ready to use.)
2. Melt butter in large saucepan or Dutch oven over medium heat. Add onion; cook and stir 3 minutes or until softened. Add flour; cook and stir 1 minute. Gradually whisk in broth until well blended.
3. Whisk in mashed potato flakes, water, half-and-half, salt, basil, thyme and pepper; bring to a boil over medium-high heat. Reduce heat to medium; cook 5 minutes.
4. Stir in baked potato cubes; cook 10 to 15 minutes or until soup is thickened and heated through. Top with cheese, bacon and green onion.

GUINNESS BEEF STEW

MAKES 6 SERVINGS

- 3 tablespoons vegetable oil, divided
- 3 pounds boneless beef chuck roast, cut into 1-inch pieces
- 2 medium onions, chopped
- 2 stalks celery, chopped
- 3 tablespoons all-purpose flour
- 1 tablespoon minced garlic
- 1 tablespoon tomato paste
- 2 teaspoons chopped fresh thyme
- 1½ teaspoons salt
- ½ teaspoon black pepper
- 1 bottle (about 15 ounces) Guinness
- 1 cup reduced-sodium beef broth
- 3 carrots, cut into 1-inch pieces
- 4 small turnips (12 ounces), peeled and cut into 1-inch pieces
- 4 medium Yukon Gold potatoes (1 pound), peeled and cut into 1-inch pieces
- ¼ cup finely chopped fresh parsley

1. Preheat oven to 350°F. Heat 2 tablespoons oil in Dutch oven over medium-high heat until almost smoking. Cook beef in two batches about 10 minutes or until browned, stirring occasionally. Remove to plate.

2. Add remaining 1 tablespoon oil to Dutch oven; heat over medium heat. Add onions and celery; cook about 10 minutes or until softened and onions are translucent, stirring occasionally.

3. Add flour, garlic, tomato paste, thyme, salt and pepper; cook and stir 1 minute. Stir in Guinness, scraping up browned bits from bottom of Dutch oven. Return beef to Dutch oven; stir in broth.

4. Cover and bake 1 hour. Stir in carrots, turnips and potatoes; cover and bake about 1 hour 20 minutes or until beef and vegetables are tender. Stir in parsley.

GREEK LEMON AND RICE SOUP

MAKES 6 TO 8 SERVINGS

- **2 tablespoons butter**
- **⅓ cup minced green onions**
- **6 cups chicken broth**
- **⅔ cup uncooked long grain rice**
- **4 eggs**
- **Juice of 1 lemon**
- **⅛ teaspoon black or white pepper (optional)**
- **Fresh mint and lemon peel (optional)**

1. Melt butter in medium saucepan over medium heat. Add green onions; cook and stir about 3 minutes or until tender.
2. Stir in broth and rice; bring to a boil over medium-high heat. Reduce heat to low; cover and simmer 20 to 25 minutes or until rice is tender.
3. Beat eggs in medium bowl. Stir in lemon juice and ½ cup hot broth mixture until blended. Gradually pour egg mixture into broth mixture in saucepan, stirring constantly. Cook and stir over low heat 2 to 3 minutes or until soup thickens enough to lightly coat spoon. *Do not boil.*
4. Stir in pepper, if desired; garnish with mint and lemon peel.

CHICKEN ENCHILADA SOUP

MAKES 8 TO 10 SERVINGS

- **2 tablespoons vegetable oil, divided**
- **1½ pounds boneless skinless chicken breasts, cut into ½-inch pieces**
- **½ cup chopped onion**
- **2 cloves garlic, minced**
- **2 cans (about 14 ounces each) chicken broth**
- **3 cups water, divided**
- **1 cup masa harina**
- **1 package (16 ounces) pasteurized process cheese product, cubed**
- **1 can (10 ounces) mild red enchilada sauce**
- **1 teaspoon chili powder**
- **½ teaspoon salt**
- **½ teaspoon ground cumin**
- **1 large tomato, seeded and chopped**
- **Crispy tortilla strips***

If tortilla strips are not available, crumble tortilla chips into bite-size pieces.

1. Heat 1 tablespoon oil in large saucepan or Dutch oven over medium-high heat. Add chicken; cook and stir 10 minutes or until no longer pink. Transfer to medium bowl with slotted spoon; drain any excess liquid from saucepan.

2. Heat remaining 1 tablespoon oil in same saucepan over medium-high heat. Add onion and garlic; cook and stir 3 minutes or until softened. Stir in broth.

3. Whisk 2 cups water into masa harina in large bowl until smooth. Whisk mixture into broth in saucepan. Stir in remaining 1 cup water, cheese product, enchilada sauce, chili powder, salt and cumin; bring to a boil over high heat. Stir in chicken. Reduce heat to medium-low; simmer 30 minutes, stirring frequently. Top with tomato and tortilla strips.

FIVE-WAY CINCINNATI CHILI

MAKES 6 SERVINGS

- 1 pound uncooked spaghetti, broken in half
- 1 pound ground beef chuck
- 2 cans (10 ounces each) tomatoes and green chiles, undrained
- 1 can (about 15 ounces) red kidney beans, drained
- 1 can (10½ ounces) condensed French onion soup, undiluted
- 1¼ cups water
- 1 tablespoon chili powder
- 1 teaspoon sugar
- ½ teaspoon salt
- ¼ teaspoon ground cinnamon
- ½ cup chopped onion
- ½ cup (2 ounces) shredded Cheddar cheese

1. Cook pasta according to package directions; drain.
2. Meanwhile, cook beef in large saucepan or Dutch oven 6 to 8 minutes over medium-high heat or until browned, stirring to break up meat. Drain fat.
3. Stir in tomatoes, beans, soup, water, chili powder, sugar, salt and cinnamon; bring to a boil. Reduce heat to low; simmer 10 minutes, stirring occasionally.
4. Serve chili over spaghetti; sprinkle with onion and cheese.

HEARTY TUSCAN SOUP

MAKES 6 TO 8 SERVINGS

- **1 teaspoon olive oil**
- **1 pound bulk mild or hot Italian sausage***
- **1 medium onion, chopped**
- **3 cloves garlic, minced**
- **¼ cup all-purpose flour**
- **5 cups chicken broth**
- **1 teaspoon salt**
- **½ teaspoon Italian seasoning**
- **3 medium unpeeled russet potatoes (about 1 pound), halved lengthwise and thinly sliced**
- **2 cups packed torn stemmed kale leaves**
- **1 cup half-and-half or whipping cream**

Or use sausage links and remove from casings.

1. Heat oil in large saucepan or Dutch oven over medium-high heat. Add sausage; cook about 8 minutes or until sausage begins to brown, stirring to break up meat.

2. Add onion and garlic; cook about 5 minutes or until onion is softened and sausage is browned, stirring occasionally.

3. Add flour; cook and stir 1 minute. Stir in broth, salt and Italian seasoning; bring to a boil. Stir in potatoes and kale. Reduce heat to medium-low; simmer 15 to 20 minutes or until potatoes are fork-tender.

4. Reduce heat to low; stir in half-and-half. Cook about 5 minutes or until heated through.

BEEFY BEER SOUP

MAKES 6 SERVINGS

- 1 tablespoon vegetable oil
- 12 ounces boneless beef round steak, cut into ½-inch pieces
- 1 large onion, chopped
- 2 medium carrots, sliced
- 2 stalks celery, chopped
- 5 cups beef broth
- 1 bottle (12 ounces) stout or dark ale
- 1 teaspoon salt
- ¾ teaspoon dried oregano
- ⅛ teaspoon black pepper
- 1 can (about 15 ounces) kidney beans, rinsed and drained
- 1 small zucchini, cut into ½-inch pieces
- 4 ounces mushrooms, sliced

1. Heat oil in large saucepan or Dutch oven over medium heat. Add beef, onion, carrots and celery; cook and stir 6 minutes or until beef is no longer pink and carrots and celery are crisp-tender.

2. Stir in broth, stout, salt, oregano and pepper; bring to a boil over high heat. Reduce heat to medium-low; simmer, uncovered, 45 minutes or until beef is fork-tender.

3. Stir in beans, zucchini and mushrooms; bring to a boil over high heat. Reduce heat to medium-low; simmer, uncovered, 5 minutes or until zucchini is tender.

ONE-POT CHINESE CHICKEN SOUP

MAKES 4 SERVINGS

- 6 cups chicken broth
- 2 cups water
- 1 pound boneless skinless chicken thighs
- ⅓ cup reduced-sodium soy sauce
- 1 package (16 ounces) frozen stir-fry vegetables
- 6 ounces uncooked dried thin Chinese egg noodles
- 1 to 3 tablespoons sriracha sauce

1. Combine broth, water, chicken and soy sauce in medium saucepan; bring to a boil over high heat. Reduce heat to low; cover and simmer 25 minutes or until chicken is cooked through and very tender. Remove chicken to plate; let stand until cool enough to handle.

2. Meanwhile, add vegetables and noodles to broth in saucepan; bring to a boil over high heat. Reduce heat to medium-high; cook 5 minutes or until noodles are tender and vegetables are heated through, stirring occasionally.

3. Shred chicken into bite-size pieces. Stir chicken and 1 tablespoon sriracha into soup; taste and add additional sriracha for a spicier flavor.

Creamy, Cheesy Pasta Perfection

LITTLE ITALY BAKED ZITI

MAKES 6 TO 8 SERVINGS

- 1 package (16 ounces) uncooked ziti pasta
- 1 pound bulk mild Italian sausage
- 3 cloves garlic, minced
- ¾ cup dry white wine
- 1 jar (24 ounces) marinara sauce
- 1 can (about 14 ounces) diced tomatoes
- 2 tablespoons butter
- 2 cups (8 ounces) shredded mozzarella cheese, divided
- ½ cup coarsely chopped fresh basil, plus additional for garnish
- ¼ cup grated Parmesan cheese

1. Cook pasta according to package directions for dente. Drain and return to saucepan; keep warm.
2. Meanwhile, cook sausage in large skillet over medium-high heat about 8 minutes or until no longer pink, stirring to break up meat. Add garlic; cook and stir 1 minute. Add wine; cook 4 minutes or until almost evaporated.
3. Stir in marinara sauce, tomatoes and butter; bring to a boil. Reduce heat to medium-low; cook 20 minutes, stirring occasionally. Preheat broiler. Spray 3-quart or 13×9-inch broilerproof baking dish with nonstick cooking spray.
4. Add sauce mixture, 1 cup mozzarella and ½ cup basil to pasta in saucepan; stir gently to coat. Spread in prepared baking dish; sprinkle with remaining 1 cup mozzarella and Parmesan.
5. Broil 2 to 3 minutes or until cheese begins to bubble and turn golden brown. Garnish with additional basil.

PUMPKIN MAC AND CHEESE

MAKES 6 TO 8 SERVINGS

- **1 package (16 ounces) uncooked large elbow macaroni or medium shell pasta**
- **½ cup (1 stick) butter, divided**
- **¼ cup all-purpose flour**
- **1½ cups milk**
- **1 teaspoon salt, divided**
- **¼ teaspoon ground nutmeg**
- **⅛ teaspoon ground red pepper**
- **2 cups (8 ounces) shredded Cheddar cheese**
- **1 cup (4 ounces) shredded Monterey Jack cheese**
- **1 cup canned pumpkin**
- **1 cup panko bread crumbs**
- **½ cup chopped hazelnuts or walnuts (optional)**
- **⅛ teaspoon dried sage**
- **1 cup (4 ounces) shredded Chihuahua cheese***

If Chihuahua cheese is not available, substitute Monterey Jack cheese.

1. Preheat oven to 350°F. Spray 2-quart baking dish with nonstick cooking spray. Cook macaroni according to package directions for al dente. Drain and return to saucepan; keep warm.

2. Melt ¼ cup butter in medium saucepan over medium-high heat. Whisk in flour until smooth; cook 1 minute without browning, whisking constantly. Gradually whisk in milk in thin, steady stream. Add ¾ teaspoon salt, nutmeg and red pepper; cook 2 to 3 minutes or until thickened, stirring frequently. Gradually add Cheddar and Monterey Jack cheeses, stirring after each addition until smooth. Add pumpkin; cook 1 minute or until heated through, stirring constantly. Pour sauce over pasta; stir to coat.

3. Melt remaining ¼ cup butter in small skillet over medium-low heat; cook until golden brown. Remove from heat; stir in panko, hazelnuts, if desired, sage and remaining ¼ teaspoon salt.

4. Spread half of pasta mixture in prepared baking dish; sprinkle with ½ cup Chihuahua cheese. Top with remaining pasta mixture; sprinkle with remaining Chihuahua cheese. Top with panko mixture.

5. Bake 25 to 30 minutes or until topping is golden brown and pasta is heated through.

VEGETABLE LO MEIN

MAKES 4 SERVINGS

- 8 ounces uncooked Chinese egg noodles or thin spaghetti
- 2 egg whites
- 1 egg
- 1 green onion, thinly sliced
- 1 teaspoon vegetable oil
- 1 tablespoon dark sesame oil
- 4 ounces shiitake mushrooms, tough stems discarded and caps sliced, *or* 1 package (4 ounces) sliced exotic mushrooms
- 2 cups thinly sliced bok choy (leaves and stems)
- 1 small red or yellow bell pepper, cut into strips
- ½ cup vegetable broth
- ¼ cup teriyaki sauce
- Chopped peanuts (optional)
- Chopped fresh cilantro (optional)

1. Cook noodles according to package directions; drain.
2. Beat egg whites and egg in small bowl until foamy. Stir in green onion. Heat vegetable oil in large nonstick skillet over medium heat. Add egg mixture; cook, without stirring, 2 to 3 minutes or until bottom is set. Gently turn omelet; cook 1 minute or until bottom is set. Transfer to cutting board. Wipe out skillet with paper towel.
3. Heat sesame oil in same skillet over medium-high heat. Add mushrooms, bok choy and bell pepper; stir-fry 4 to 5 minutes or until vegetables are tender. Add broth and teriyaki sauce; cook and stir 2 minutes. Remove to large bowl. Add noodles; toss to coat.
4. Cut omelet into strips. Add to noodle mixture; stir gently to combine. Sprinkle with peanuts and cilantro, if desired.

TURKEY BURGER CASSEROLE

MAKES 6 TO 8 SERVINGS

- 1 package (16 ounces) uncooked orecchiette pasta
- 1 tablespoon vegetable oil
- 1 pound ground turkey
- 1 medium onion, chopped
- 1 clove garlic, minced
- 1 teaspoon salt
- ¼ teaspoon black pepper
- 2 tablespoons ketchup
- 1 tablespoon yellow mustard
- 1 can (28 ounces) diced tomatoes
- 2 cups (8 ounces) shredded Cheddar cheese, divided
- 4 slices bacon, cooked and chopped (optional)
- Optional toppings: shredded lettuce, sliced onion, sliced tomatoes and/or dill pickle slices

1. Preheat oven to 350°F. Spray 13×9-inch baking dish with nonstick cooking spray.

2. Cook pasta according to package directions for al dente. Drain pasta and place in large bowl, reserving ¼ cup cooking water.

3. Meanwhile, heat oil in large skillet over medium-high heat. Add turkey, onion, garlic, salt and pepper; cook about 8 minutes or until turkey is no longer pink, stirring to break up meat.

4. Stir in ketchup and mustard; mix well. Stir in tomatoes and reserved pasta water; bring to a simmer. Add turkey mixture to pasta; mix well. Stir in ½ cup cheese. Spread in prepared baking dish; top with remaining 1½ cups cheese.

5. Bake about 20 minutes or until cheese is melted and casserole is heated through. Sprinkle with bacon, if desired; let stand 5 minutes. Serve with desired toppings.

CLASSIC LASAGNA

MAKES 6 TO 8 SERVINGS

- 1 tablespoon olive oil
- 8 ounces bulk mild Italian sausage
- 8 ounces ground beef
- 1 medium onion, chopped
- 3 cloves garlic, minced, divided
- 1½ teaspoons salt, divided
- 1 can (28 ounces) crushed tomatoes
- 1 can (28 ounces) diced tomatoes
- 2 teaspoons Italian seasoning
- 1 egg
- 1 container (15 ounces) ricotta cheese
- ¾ cup grated Parmesan cheese, divided
- ½ cup minced fresh parsley
- ¼ teaspoon black pepper
- 12 uncooked no-boil lasagna noodles
- 4 cups (16 ounces) shredded mozzarella

1. Preheat oven to 350°F. Spray 13×9-inch baking dish with nonstick cooking spray.

2. Heat oil in large saucepan over medium-high heat. Add sausage, beef, onion, 2 cloves garlic and 1 teaspoon salt; cook and stir 10 minutes or until meat is no longer pink, stirring to break up meat. Add crushed tomatoes, diced tomatoes and Italian seasoning; bring to a boil. Reduce heat to medium-low; cook 15 minutes, stirring occasionally.

3. Meanwhile, beat egg in medium bowl. Stir in ricotta, ½ cup Parmesan, parsley, remaining 1 clove garlic, ½ teaspoon salt and pepper until well blended.

4. Spread ¼ cup sauce in prepared baking dish. Top with 3 noodles, breaking to fit if necessary. Spread one third of ricotta mixture over noodles. Sprinkle with 1 cup mozzarella; top with 2 cups sauce. Repeat layers of noodles, ricotta mixture, mozzarella and sauce two times. Top with remaining 3 noodles, sauce, 1 cup mozzarella and ¼ cup Parmesan. Cover dish with foil sprayed with cooking spray.

5. Bake 30 minutes. Remove foil; bake 10 to 15 minutes or until hot and bubbly. Let stand 10 minutes before serving.

PERFECT MAC AND CHEESE

MAKES 6 TO 8 SERVINGS

- **1 package (16 ounces) uncooked elbow macaroni**
- **¼ cup (½ stick) butter**
- **¼ cup all-purpose flour**
- **3 cups whole milk**
- **1 teaspoon salt**
- **¼ teaspoon black pepper**
- **4 cups (16 ounces) shredded Cheddar cheese, divided**
- **Fresh basil leaves (optional)**

1 Preheat oven to 400°F. Spray 6 to 8 (1-cup) ramekins with nonstick cooking spray.*

2 Cook pasta according to package directions for al dente; drain and set aside.

3 Melt butter in large saucepan over medium heat. Add flour; whisk until well blended and bubbly. Slowly add milk, salt and pepper, whisking until blended. Cook and stir until milk begins to bubble.

4 Reduce heat to low. Slowly add 3½ cups cheese; cook and stir until cheese is melted and sauce is smooth. Add cooked pasta; stir gently until blended. Spoon into prepared ramekins; sprinkle with remaining ½ cup cheese.

5 Bake about 20 minutes or until bubbly and golden brown. Garnish with basil.

**Or use 3-quart baking dish; prepare recipe as directed and bake 25 to 30 minutes.*

CHICKEN TETRAZZINI CASSEROLE

MAKES 4 SERVINGS

- **8 ounces uncooked vermicelli pasta, broken in half**
- **1 can (10¾ ounces) condensed cream of mushroom soup, undiluted**
- **¼ cup half-and-half**
- **3 tablespoons dry sherry**
- **½ teaspoon salt**
- **⅛ to ¼ teaspoon red pepper flakes**
- **2 cups chopped cooked chicken**
- **1 cup frozen peas**
- **½ cup grated Parmesan cheese**
- **1 cup coarse fresh bread crumbs**
- **2 tablespoons butter, melted**

1. Preheat oven to 375°F. Spray 8-inch square baking dish with nonstick cooking spray.
2. Cook pasta according to package directions for al dente; drain.
3. Meanwhile, combine soup, half-and-half, sherry, salt and red pepper flakes in large bowl. Stir in chicken, peas and cheese. Add pasta; stir until well coated. Transfer to prepared baking dish.
4. Combine bread crumbs and butter in small bowl; sprinkle over casserole.
5. Bake 25 to 30 minutes or until heated through and crumbs are golden brown.

CHILI AND CHEDDAR BAKED MACARONI

MAKES 8 SERVINGS

- 1 pound ground beef or turkey
- 1 can (8 ounces) tomato sauce
- 1 small onion, diced
- 1 jalapeño pepper, seeded and minced
- 1 package (about 1 ounce) chili seasoning mix
- 1 cup water
- 1 package (16 ounces) uncooked elbow macaroni
- 2 cups (8 ounces) shredded sharp Cheddar cheese

1. Cook beef in large skillet over medium-high heat 6 to 8 minutes or until browned, stirring to break up meat. Drain fat.

2. Stir in tomato sauce, onion, jalapeño and chili seasoning. Stir in water; bring to a boil. Reduce heat to low; simmer about 45 minutes or until chili is thick.

3. Meanwhile, cook macaroni according to package directions for al dente; drain and return to saucepan.

4. Preheat oven to 400°F. Spray 9-inch square baking dish with nonstick cooking spray. Spread one third of macaroni in baking dish; top with one third of chili and one third of cheese. Repeat layers twice.

5. Bake 30 to 35 minutes or until edges begin to brown. Cool 5 to 10 minutes before serving.

CREAMY HERBED NOODLES WITH ROASTED TOMATOES

MAKES 6 SERVINGS

- **1 pint grape tomatoes, halved**
- **1 tablespoon olive oil**
- **¾ teaspoon salt, divided**
- **2 tablespoons butter**
- **1 clove garlic, smashed**
- **2 tablespoons all-purpose flour**
- **2 cups half-and-half, heated**
- **8 ounces good-quality ripe Brie, crust removed, cut into small chunks**
- **¼ cup finely chopped fresh basil**
- **2 tablespoons minced fresh chives**
- **¼ teaspoon pepper**
- **6 ounces egg noodles, cooked (3½ to 4 cups uncooked)**
- **¼ cup sliced almonds**

1. Preheat oven to 425°F. Line baking sheet with heavy-duty foil. Spray 9-inch square baking dish with nonstick cooking spray.

2. Spread tomatoes on prepared baking sheet; drizzle with oil and sprinkle with ¼ teaspoon salt. Roast 20 minutes or until tomatoes are tender and slightly shriveled. Set aside. *Reduce oven temperature to 350°F.*

3. Melt butter in large saucepan or deep skillet over medium heat. Add garlic clove; cook 1 minute. Whisk in flour until blended. Gradually add half-and-half; cook until thickened, whisking constantly. Remove and discard garlic. Gradually stir in cheese until melted.

4. Add basil, chives, remaining ½ teaspoon salt and pepper; mix well. Add noodles; stir gently to coat. Drain off any liquid from tomatoes; fold into noodle mixture. Transfer to prepared baking dish.

5. Bake 17 to 20 minutes or until sauce begins to bubble. Sprinkle with almonds; bake 8 to 10 minutes or until nuts are lightly browned.

CHEESY ITALIAN RAMEN CASSEROLE

MAKES 8 TO 10 SERVINGS

- **4 packages (3 ounces each) ramen noodles***
- **1 pound sweet Italian sausage, casings removed**
- **1 cup diced onion**
- **1 cup diced red bell pepper**
- **1 teaspoon minced garlic**
- **1 can (about 15 ounces) tomato sauce**
- **½ cup thinly sliced fresh basil**
- **2 cups (8 ounces) shredded mozzarella cheese**

Use any flavor; discard seasoning packets.

1. Preheat oven to 400°F. Spray 13×9-inch baking dish with nonstick cooking spray.

2. Cook noodles according to package directions; drain and rinse under cold water to stop cooking. Transfer to large bowl.

3. Cook sausage in large skillet over medium-high heat 6 to 8 minutes or until browned, stirring to break up meat. Drain on paper towel-lined plate. Add to bowl with noodles.

4. Add onion and bell pepper to skillet; cook and stir 6 minutes or until vegetables are softened. Add garlic; cook and stir 30 seconds. Add vegetable mixture, tomato sauce and basil to bowl with noodles; stir to coat. Spread in prepared baking dish; sprinkle with cheese.

5. Bake 25 to 30 minutes or until bubbly and cheese is melted. Let stand 5 minutes before serving.

PARMESAN ALFREDO PASTA BAKE

MAKES 6 TO 8 SERVINGS

- **2 tablespoons plus ½ teaspoon salt, divided**
- **1 package (16 ounces) uncooked fusilli pasta**
- **6 tablespoons (¾ stick) butter**
- **1 clove garlic, smashed**
- **1 cup whipping cream**
- **1 cup milk**
- **2 cups shredded Parmesan cheese, divided**
- **1 cup (4 ounces) shredded mozzarella cheese**
- **4 ounces mozzarella cheese, cubed**
- **1 cup panko bread crumbs**
- **2 tablespoons butter, melted**
- **¼ teaspoon Italian seasoning**

1 Preheat oven to 400°F. Spray 3-quart baking dish with nonstick cooking spray.

2 Bring large saucepan of water to a boil; stir in 2 tablespoons salt. Add pasta; cook according to package directions for al dente. Drain pasta, reserving ½ cup cooking water. Return pasta to saucepan.

3 Meanwhile, melt 6 tablespoons butter in medium saucepan over medium heat. Add garlic and remaining ½ teaspoon salt; cook and stir 1 minute. Stir in cream, milk and reserved ½ cup pasta water; bring to a simmer. Remove from heat; remove and discard garlic. Gradually stir in 1 cup Parmesan and shredded mozzarella until sauce is smooth and well blended. Pour over pasta; stir gently to coat. Fold in cubed mozzarella; transfer to prepared baking dish.

4 Combine panko, remaining 1 cup Parmesan and 2 tablespoons melted butter in medium bowl; mix well. Spread evenly over pasta mixture; sprinkle with Italian seasoning.

5 Bake 15 minutes or until topping is golden brown and pasta is heated through.

SMOKED SAUSAGE MAC AND CHEESE

MAKES 6 TO 8 SERVINGS

- 1 tablespoon olive oil
- 1 medium onion, finely chopped
- 1 package (about 12 ounces) smoked turkey sausage, cut into ¼-inch slices
- 1 package (16 ounces) uncooked cavatappi pasta
- 4 cups water
- 2 teaspoons salt, divided
- 4 tablespoons (½ stick) butter, divided
- 1 clove garlic, minced
- 1 cup panko bread crumbs
- 4 cups (16 ounces) shredded Cheddar cheese
- 1 cup (4 ounces) shredded Monterey Jack cheese
- 1 cup evaporated milk
- Black pepper

1. Heat oil in large saucepan or Dutch oven over medium-high heat. Add onion; cook 5 to 7 minutes or until golden brown. Add sausage; cook and stir 5 minutes or until lightly browned.

2. Add pasta, water and 1½ teaspoons salt; cover and cook 13 to 15 minutes or until pasta is al dente, stirring occasionally.

3. Meanwhile, melt 2 tablespoons butter in medium skillet over medium-high heat. Add garlic; cook and stir 30 seconds. Add panko and remaining ½ teaspoon salt; cook and stir 2 minutes or until panko is golden brown. Remove from heat.

4. Uncover pasta and reduce heat to medium-low. Stir in Cheddar, Monterey Jack, evaporated milk and remaining 2 tablespoons butter; cook and stir 1 to 2 minutes or until cheese is melted and pasta is creamy. Season with pepper; sprinkle with panko mixture. Serve immediately.

SPAGHETTI AND MEATBALLS

MAKES 4 SERVINGS

- 12 ounces ground beef
- 4 ounces hot Italian sausages, casings removed
- 1 egg white
- 2 tablespoons plain dry bread crumbs
- 1 teaspoon dried oregano
- ½ teaspoon salt
- 2 cups tomato-basil pasta sauce
- 8 ounces uncooked spaghetti
- 2 tablespoons chopped fresh basil
- 2 tablespoons grated Parmesan cheese

1. Preheat oven to 450°F. Spray baking sheet with nonstick cooking spray.
2. Combine beef, sausage, egg white, bread crumbs, oregano and salt in medium bowl; mix well. Shape mixture into 16 (1½-inch) meatballs. Place on prepared baking sheet; spray with cooking spray. Bake 12 minutes, turning once.
3. Pour pasta sauce into large skillet. Add meatballs; cook over medium heat 9 minutes or until sauce is heated through and meatballs are cooked through (160°F), stirring occasionally.
4. Meanwhile, cook spaghetti according to package directions. Drain spaghetti; top with meatballs and sauce. Sprinkle with basil and cheese.

BAKED PASTA AND CHEESE SUPREME

MAKES 4 SERVINGS

- 8 ounces uncooked fusilli pasta or other corkscrew-shaped pasta
- 12 slices bacon, chopped
- ½ medium onion, chopped
- 2 cloves garlic, minced
- 2 teaspoons dried oregano, divided
- 1 can (8 ounces) tomato sauce
- 1 teaspoon hot pepper sauce (optional)
- 1½ cups (6 ounces) shredded Cheddar or Colby cheese
- ½ cup fresh bread crumbs (from 1 slice of white bread)
- 1 tablespoon butter, melted

1. Preheat oven to 400°F. Cook pasta according to package directions for al dente; drain.
2. Meanwhile, cook bacon in large ovenproof skillet over medium heat until crisp. Drain on paper towel-lined plate.
3. Add onion, garlic and 1 teaspoon oregano to skillet; cook and stir 3 minutes or until onion is translucent. Stir in tomato sauce and hot pepper sauce, if desired. Add pasta and cheese; stir to coat.
4. Combine bacon, bread crumbs, remaining 1 teaspoon oregano and butter in small bowl; sprinkle over pasta mixture.
5. Bake 10 to 15 minutes or until hot and bubbly.

Substantial Sandwiches + Pizza

ITALIAN BEEF SANDWICHES

MAKES 6 TO 8 SERVINGS

- 1 jar (12 ounces) sliced pepperoncini peppers
- 1 jar (16 ounces) giardiniera
- 3 pounds boneless beef chuck roast
- 1 teaspoon salt
- ½ teaspoon black pepper
- 1 tablespoon olive oil
- 1 can (about 15 ounces) beef broth, divided
- 2 teaspoons Italian seasoning
- 6 French or sub rolls, split

1. Preheat oven to 325°F. Set aside ½ cup pepperoncini for sandwiches, leaving liquid in jar. Drain giardiniera; set aside ¾ cup vegetables for sandwiches. Cut beef into four pieces; season with salt and pepper.

2. Heat oil in Dutch oven over medium-high heat. Add beef; cook 8 to 10 minutes per side or until well browned. Remove to plate. Drain fat. Add ¼ cup broth to Dutch oven; cook and stir 1 minute, scraping up browned bits from bottom of pan. Stir in remaining broth, remaining pepperoncini with liquid, remaining giardiniera vegetables and Italian seasoning; bring to a boil. Return beef to Dutch oven. (Beef should be about half submerged in liquid; add water if necessary.)

3. Cover and bake 2½ to 3 hours or until beef is tender. Remove beef to large bowl; let stand until cool enough to handle.

4. Shred beef into bite-size pieces. Add ¾ cup cooking liquid; toss to coat.

5. Fill rolls with beef, reserved pepperoncini and giardiniera vegetables. Serve with remaining warm cooking liquid for dipping.

PULLED PORK SANDWICHES >

MAKES 6 TO 8 SERVINGS

- 2 tablespoons coarse salt
- 2 tablespoons packed brown sugar
- 2 tablespoons paprika
- 1 teaspoon dry mustard
- 1 teaspoon black pepper
- 1 boneless pork shoulder roast (about 3 pounds)
- 1½ cups stout
- ½ cup cider vinegar
- 6 to 8 Kaiser rolls or hamburger buns, split
- ¾ cup barbecue sauce

1. Preheat oven to 325°F. Combine salt, brown sugar, paprika, mustard and pepper in small bowl; mix well. Rub into pork.
2. Place pork in Dutch oven; add stout and vinegar. Cover and bake 3 hours or until meat is fork-tender.
3. Remove pork to cutting board; let stand 15 to 30 minutes or until cool enough to handle. Shred pork into bite-size pieces with two forks. Serve pork on rolls; top with barbecue sauce.

GRILLED 3-CHEESE SANDWICHES

MAKES 2 SERVINGS

- 2 slices (1 ounce each) Muenster cheese
- 2 slices (1 ounce each) Swiss cheese
- 2 slices (1 ounce each) Cheddar cheese
- 4 slices sourdough bread
- 2 teaspoons Dijon mustard or Dijon mustard mayonnaise
- 1 tablespoon butter, melted

1. Place one slice of each cheese on two bread slices. Spread mustard over cheese; top with remaining bread slices. Brush outsides of sandwiches with butter.
2. Heat large skillet over medium heat. Add sandwiches; press down lightly with spatula or weigh down with small plate. Cook 4 minutes per side or until cheese is melted and sandwiches are golden brown.

CLASSIC MUSHROOM PIZZA

MAKES 8 SERVINGS (2 PIZZAS)

- 3 to 3½ cups all-purpose flour
- 1¼ cups warm water (120°F)
- 3 tablespoons olive oil, divided
- 1 package (¼ ounce) instant yeast
- 1¼ teaspoons salt, divided
- 8 to 10 medium mushrooms, cut into ⅛-inch-thick slices
- ⅛ teaspoon black pepper
- 1 cup pizza sauce, divided
- 3 cups (12 ounces) shredded mozzarella cheese, divided
- Pinch dried oregano and red pepper flakes
- Fresh thyme or chopped fresh basil (optional)

1. Combine 3 cups flour, water, 2 tablespoons oil, yeast and 1 teaspoon salt in large bowl of stand mixer. Mix with dough hook at low speed about 2 minutes or until soft dough forms, adding additional flour, 1 tablespoon at a time, if necessary to clean side of bowl. Mix at medium-low speed 5 minutes.

2. Shape dough into a ball. Place dough in greased bowl; turn to grease top. Cover and let rise in warm place about 1 hour or until doubled in size.

3. Preheat oven to 500°F. Combine mushrooms, 1 teaspoon oil, remaining ¼ teaspoon salt and pepper in small bowl; toss to coat.

4. Gently punch down dough; turn out onto lightly floured surface. Divide dough in half; keep one half covered to prevent drying out. Roll out remaining half of dough into 12-inch circle; transfer to pizza pan or baking sheet.

5. Brush edge of dough with 1 teaspoon oil. Spread ½ cup sauce over dough, leaving ¼-inch border. Sprinkle with 1½ cups cheese; top with half of mushrooms. Sprinkle with oregano and red pepper flakes.

6. Bake about 10 minutes or until crust is golden brown and cheese is melted. Sprinkle with fresh herbs, if desired; remove to wire rack to cool 5 minutes. While pizza is baking, roll out and top remaining half of dough with remaining oil, sauce, cheese and mushrooms.

CLASSIC PATTY MELTS

MAKES 4 SERVINGS

- 5 tablespoons butter, divided
- 2 large yellow onions, thinly sliced
- ¾ teaspoon plus pinch of salt, divided
- 1 pound ground beef chuck (80% lean)
- ½ teaspoon garlic powder
- ½ teaspoon onion powder
- ¼ teaspoon black pepper
- 8 slices marble rye bread
- ½ cup Thousand Island dressing
- 8 slices (about 1 ounce each) deli American or Swiss cheese

1. Melt 2 tablespoons butter in large skillet over medium heat. Add onions and pinch of salt; cook 20 minutes or until onions are very soft and golden brown, stirring occasionally. Remove to small bowl; wipe out skillet with paper towel.

2. Combine beef, remaining ¾ teaspoon salt, garlic powder, onion powder and pepper in medium bowl; mix gently. Shape into four patties about the size and shape of bread slices and ¼ to ½ inch thick.

3. Melt 1 tablespoon butter in same skillet over medium-high heat. Add patties, two at a time; cook 3 minutes or until bottoms are browned, pressing down gently with spatula to form crust. Turn patties; cook 3 minutes or until browned. Remove patties to plate; wipe out skillet with paper towel.

4. Spread one side of each bread slice with dressing. Top four bread slices with cheese slice, patty, caramelized onions, another cheese slice and remaining bread slices.

5. Melt 1 tablespoon butter in same skillet over medium heat. Add two sandwiches to skillet; cook 4 minutes or until golden brown, pressing down with spatula to crisp bread. Turn sandwiches; cook 4 minutes or until golden brown and cheese is melted. Repeat with remaining 1 tablespoon butter and sandwiches.

CHICKEN SAUSAGE, FENNEL AND APPLE FLATBREAD

MAKES 6 SERVINGS

- 2 tablespoons sun-dried tomato or balsamic vinaigrette
- 1 (10½-ounce) stone-baked pizza crust*
- 1 small red onion, thinly sliced
- ½ fennel bulb, thinly sliced
- 1 fully-cooked sun-dried tomato chicken sausage, thinly sliced
- 1 Granny Smith apple, peeled and thinly sliced
- ¾ cup finely shredded mozzarella cheese
- 2 tablespoons grated Parmesan cheese

**Or substitute standard 12-inch prepared pizza crust.*

1. Preheat oven to 400°F. Spread dressing over pizza crust.
2. Top with onion, fennel, sausage and apple; sprinkle with mozzarella and Parmesan.
3. Bake 20 minutes or until cheese is melted and crust is golden brown.

BACON-TOMATO GRILLED CHEESE >

MAKES 4 SERVINGS

- 8 slices bacon, cut in half
- 4 slices sharp Cheddar cheese
- 4 slices Gouda cheese
- 4 tomato slices
- 8 slices whole wheat or white bread
- 2 tablespoons butter

1 Cook bacon in large skillet over medium-high heat until crisp; remove to paper towel-lined plate. Drain off drippings; wipe out skillet with paper towels.

2 Layer one Cheddar slice, one Gouda slice, one tomato slice and two bacon slices on each of four bread slices; top with remaining bread slices.

3 Melt 1 tablespoon butter in same skillet over medium heat. Add two sandwiches; cook 4 minutes or until bottoms are browned. Turn sandwiches. Reduce heat to medium-low; cover and cook 3 to 4 minutes or until bottoms are browned and cheese is melted. Repeat with remaining sandwiches and butter.

FIESTA CHICKEN SANDWICH

MAKES 4 SERVINGS

- 2 tablespoons olive oil, plus additional for brushing sandwiches
- 1 small onion, sliced
- 1 red bell pepper, sliced
- 12 ounces chicken tenders, cut in half lengthwise and crosswise
- 1 cup guacamole
- 4 slices (1 ounce each) pepper Jack cheese
- 2 packages (10 ounces each) 8-inch mini pizza crusts (8 total)

1 Heat 2 tablespoons oil in large skillet over medium-high heat. Add onion and bell pepper; cook and stir 4 minutes or until vegetables are crisp-tender. Remove to plate. Add chicken to skillet; cook and stir 4 minutes or until cooked through. Remove to plate; wipe out skillet with paper towel.

2 Layer guacamole, chicken, vegetables and cheese on four pizza crusts; top with remaining four crusts. Brush sandwiches lightly with additional oil.

3 Heat same skillet over medium heat. Cook sandwiches in batches 4 to 5 minutes per side or until cheese melts and sandwiches are golden brown. Cut into wedges.

MAC AND CHEESE PIZZA

MAKES 4 TO 6 SERVINGS

- 1½ tablespoons butter
- 1½ tablespoons all-purpose flour
- 1 cup half-and-half or milk, heated
- ¼ teaspoon salt
- ¼ teaspoon black pepper
- ¼ teaspoon dried oregano
- ½ cup shredded fontina cheese
- ½ cup shredded Parmesan cheese
- 3 cups cooked* macaroni (about 1½ cups uncooked)
- 1 tablespoon olive oil
- 1 cup sliced mushrooms
- 8 ounces mild bulk Italian sausage
- 1 cup marinara sauce
- 1 cup (4 ounces) shredded mozzarella cheese

**Cook macaroni until very tender, slightly longer than for al dente pasta.*

1 Preheat oven to 350°F. Spray 10-inch deep-dish pizza pan, tart pan or shallow casserole with nonstick cooking spray.

2 Melt butter in large saucepan over medium-low heat until bubbly. Whisk in flour until smooth paste forms. Gradually whisk in half-and-half until thickened. Add salt, pepper and oregano. Gradually stir in fontina and Parmesan until melted. Stir in macaroni. Spread in prepared pan; press down firmly into even layer. Bake 15 minutes.

3 Meanwhile, heat oil in large skillet over medium heat. Add mushrooms; cook 5 minutes, stirring occasionally. Increase heat to medium-high. Add sausage; cook until browned, stirring to break up meat. Drain fat.

4 Stir in marinara sauce; cook 1 minute or until heated through. Spread sauce mixture evenly over baked pasta crust; sprinkle with mozzarella.

5 Bake 15 to 20 minutes, or until topping is bubbly and cheese is melted. Let stand 5 minutes before slicing.

MUSHROOM CHEESESTEAK SANDWICHES

MAKES 4 SERVINGS

- 8 ounces mushrooms, cut into ½-inch slices
- 1½ teaspoons salt, divided
- 2 tablespoons vegetable oil, divided
- 1 medium onion, cut into ½-inch slices
- 1 green bell pepper, cut into ½-inch slices
- ½ teaspoon garlic powder
- ½ teaspoon black pepper, divided
- 1 pound skirt or flank steak
- 4 French bread or hoagie rolls, split and toasted
- 8 slices provolone cheese

1. Place mushrooms in dry large skillet;* add ¾ teaspoon salt and cook over medium-high heat about 5 minutes or until mushrooms release their liquid and begin to brown, stirring occasionally.

2. Add 1 tablespoon oil, onion, bell pepper, garlic powder and ¼ teaspoon black pepper to skillet; cook 6 to 8 minutes or until vegetables begin to brown, stirring occasionally.

3. While vegetables are cooking, cut steak in half lengthwise, then cut crosswise (against the grain) into ¼-inch slices. Season with remaining ¾ teaspoon salt and ¼ teaspoon black pepper.

4. Remove vegetables to medium bowl; cover to keep warm. Heat remaining 1 tablespoon oil in same skillet over medium-high heat. Add steak in single layer; cook 1 to 2 minutes per side or just until edges are browned. Add steak and any juices in skillet to vegetables in bowl; stir to blend.

5. Spoon one fourth of steak and vegetable mixture onto bottom of each roll; top with two cheese slices. If desired, cover sandwiches loosely with foil and let stand briefly to melt cheese, or place sandwiches in low oven to melt cheese.

**For better browning of steak and vegetables, do not use a nonstick skillet.*

BBQ CHICKEN SKILLET PIZZA

MAKES 4 TO 6 SERVINGS

- 1 tablespoon olive oil
- 2 cups shredded cooked chicken*
- ¾ cup barbecue sauce, divided
- 1 loaf (16 ounces) frozen bread dough, thawed according to package directions
- ¼ cup (1 ounce) shredded mozzarella cheese
- ¼ cup thinly sliced red onion
- ½ cup (2 ounces) shredded smoked Gouda cheese
- Chopped fresh cilantro (optional)

***Use a rotisserie chicken for best flavor and convenience.**

1. Preheat oven to 425°F. Brush oil over bottom and side of large (12-inch) cast iron skillet; place in oven 5 minutes to preheat.
2. Combine chicken and ½ cup barbecue sauce in medium bowl; toss to coat.
3. Roll out dough into 15-inch circle on lightly floured surface. Remove hot skillet from oven; press dough into bottom and about 1 inch up side of skillet.
4. Spread remaining ¼ cup barbecue sauce over dough. Sprinkle with mozzarella; top with chicken mixture. Sprinkle with half of onion and Gouda; top with remaining onion.
5. Bake 25 minutes or until crust is golden brown. Garnish with cilantro.

PERFECT GRILLED REUBENS >

MAKES 4 SERVINGS

- 2 cups sauerkraut
- ¼ cup (½ stick) butter, softened
- 8 slices marble rye or rye bread
- 12 ounces thinly sliced deli corned beef or pastrami
- ¼ to ½ cup Thousand Island dressing
- 4 slices Swiss cheese
- Coleslaw (optional)

1. Preheat grill pan or panini press. Drain sauerkraut well on paper towels.
2. Spread butter evenly over one side of each bread slice. Turn four slices over; top evenly with corned beef, 1 to 2 tablespoons dressing, sauerkraut and cheese. Top with remaining four bread slices, butter side up.
3. Grill sandwiches 4 minutes or just until bread is golden brown and cheese begins to melt. Serve with coleslaw, if desired.

Tip

Stack the sandwich ingredients in the order given to prevent sogginess.

PEAR GORGONZOLA MELTS

MAKES 4 SERVINGS

- 4 ounces creamy Gorgonzola cheese (do not use crumbled blue cheese)
- 8 slices walnut raisin bread
- 2 pears, cored and sliced
- ½ cup fresh spinach leaves
- 2 tablespoons butter, melted

1. Spread cheese on four bread slices. Layer with pears and spinach; top with remaining four bread slices. Brush outsides of sandwiches with butter.
2. Heat large skillet over medium heat. Cook sandwiches in batches 4 to 5 minutes per side or until cheese is melted and sandwiches are golden brown.

FRENCH DIP SANDWICHES

MAKES 6 SERVINGS

- 3 pounds boneless beef chuck roast
- ½ teaspoon salt
- ½ teaspoon black pepper
- 1 tablespoon olive oil
- 2 large onions, cut into halves, then cut into ¼-inch slices
- 2¼ cups reduced-sodium beef broth, divided
- 3 tablespoons Worcestershire sauce
- 6 hoagie rolls, split
- 12 slices provolone cheese

1. Season beef with salt and pepper. Heat oil in Dutch oven or large saucepan over medium-high heat. Add beef; cook about 6 minutes per side or until browned. Remove to plate.

2. Add onions and ¼ cup broth to Dutch oven; cook 10 minutes or until golden brown, stirring occasionally and scraping up browned bits from bottom of pot. Remove half of onions to small bowl; set aside for serving.

3. Stir in remaining 2 cups broth and Worcestershire sauce; mix well. Return beef to Dutch oven. Reduce heat to low; cover and cook 3 to 3½ hours or until beef is fork-tender.

4. Remove beef to large bowl; let stand until cool enough to handle. Shred into bite-size pieces. Add ⅔ cup cooking liquid; toss to coat. Pour remaining cooking liquid into small bowl for serving. Preheat broiler. Line baking sheet with foil.

5. Place rolls cut side up on prepared baking sheet; broil until lightly browned. Top bottom halves of rolls with cheese, beef and reserved onions. Serve with warm au jus for dipping.

MEXICAN PIZZA

MAKES 4 SERVINGS

- 1 pound ground beef
- ¾ cup water
- 1 package (about 1 ounce) taco seasoning mix
- 1 to 2 tablespoons vegetable oil
- 8 (8-inch) flour tortillas
- 1 can (15 ounces) refried beans
- 1 cup taco sauce, divided
- 1⅓ cups shredded Colby Jack or Mexican blend cheese
- Optional toppings: diced fresh tomato, sliced black olives, sliced green onions, shredded lettuce

1. Preheat oven to 400°F. Line baking sheet with parchment paper.
2. Cook beef in medium skillet over medium-high heat 6 to 8 minutes or until browned, stirring to break up meat. Drain fat. Stir in water and taco seasoning. Reduce heat to medium-low; cook about 10 minutes or until most of liquid is absorbed, stirring occasionally.
3. Meanwhile, heat 1 tablespoon oil in large skillet over medium-high heat. Cook tortillas in batches about 2 minutes per side or until crisp and lightly browned, adding additional oil if necessary. Drain on paper towel-lined plate. Arrange four tortillas on prepared baking sheet.
4. Heat refried beans in microwave or on stovetop according to package directions. Spread one fourth of beans (heaping ⅓ cup) on each tortilla on baking sheet. Top with one fourth of beef mixture (scant ½ cup); drizzle with 1 tablespoon taco sauce. Place remaining tortillas over beef mixture. Spread 3 tablespoons taco sauce over each tortilla; sprinkle with ⅓ cup cheese.
5. Bake 4 to 5 minutes or until cheese is melted. Immediately sprinkle with desired toppings. Cut into quarters.

HAM AND EGG PANINI

MAKES 2 SERVINGS

- 1 tablespoon butter
- ¼ cup chopped red or green bell pepper
- 2 tablespoons sliced green onion
- 1 slice (1 ounce) smoked deli ham, chopped
- 2 eggs
- ¼ teaspoon salt
- ⅛ teaspoon black pepper
- 4 slices multigrain or whole grain bread
- 2 slices Cheddar or Swiss cheese

1. Melt butter in small skillet over medium heat. Add bell pepper and green onion; cook and stir 4 minutes or until vegetables are crisp-tender. Stir in ham.

2. Beat eggs, salt and black pepper in small bowl. Pour egg mixture into skillet; cook 2 minutes or until egg mixture is almost set, stirring occasionally.

3. Heat grill pan or medium skillet over medium heat. Spray one side of each bread slice with nonstick cooking spray; turn bread over. Top two bread slices with one cheese slice, half of egg mixture and remaining bread slices.

4. Grill sandwiches 2 minutes per side or until bread is toasted, pressing down lightly with spatula. (Cover pan with lid during last 2 minutes of cooking to melt cheese, if desired.) Serve immediately.

PULLED CHICKEN SANDWICHES

MAKES 4 SERVINGS

- 1 cup water
- 1 cup barbecue sauce, divided
- 2 tablespoons Worcestershire sauce
- 2 pounds boneless skinless chicken thighs
- 1 small red onion, cut in half and thinly sliced
- 4 pretzel rolls or sandwich buns, split
- ½ cup cabbage slaw

1 Combine water, ¾ cup barbecue sauce and Worcestershire sauce in large saucepan; mix well. Add chicken and onion; stir to blend. (Liquid should just cover chicken; add additional water if necessary.) Bring to a simmer over medium-high heat.

2 Reduce heat to medium-low; cover and simmer 35 minutes or until chicken is cooked through (165°F). Remove chicken to medium bowl; let stand 10 to 15 minutes or until cool enough to handle.

3 Meanwhile, cook liquid in saucepan over medium-high heat 10 to 15 minutes or until reduced by half.

4 Shred chicken into bite-size pieces in bowl. Add remaining ¼ cup barbecue sauce and ¼ cup reduced cooking liquid; toss to coat. (Serve remaining cooking liquid for dipping, if desired.)

5 Serve chicken on rolls with cabbage slaw.

DEEP DISH SAUSAGE AND SPINACH PIZZA

MAKES 4 TO 6 SERVINGS

- 1 loaf (16 ounces) frozen bread dough, thawed according to package directions
- 8 ounces bulk Italian sausage
- ⅔ cup pizza sauce
- 1½ cups (6 ounces) shredded mozzarella cheese
- 1 package (10 ounces) frozen chopped spinach, thawed and squeezed dry
- ½ cup grated Parmesan cheese

1. Spray clean work surface with nonstick cooking spray. Roll out dough into 12-inch circle; cover with plastic wrap and let rest 30 minutes.
2. Meanwhile, cook sausage in medium skillet over medium-high heat 10 minutes or until browned, stirring to break up meat. Drain fat. Stir in pizza sauce.
3. Preheat oven to 450°F. Position oven rack near bottom of oven. Spray 9-inch cake pan with cooking spray.
4. Place dough in prepared pan, pressing into bottom and 1 to 1½ inches up side of pan. Sprinkle half of mozzarella over dough; layer with half of sausage mixture, half of spinach, half of Parmesan, remaining half of sausage mixture and spinach. Top with remaining mozzarella and Parmesan.
5. Bake 15 to 18 minutes or until crust is golden brown and cheese is melted and beginning to brown in spots. Cool in pan on wire rack 5 minutes before cutting into wedges.

MEXICAN PORK SANDWICHES

MAKES 8 SERVINGS

- Juice of 1 lime
- 1 tablespoon olive oil
- 4 cloves garlic, minced
- 1 teaspoon black pepper
- ½ teaspoon salt
- 2 onions, thinly sliced
- 2 jalapeño peppers, seeded and thinly sliced
- 1 pork tenderloin (2 pounds)
- 8 French rolls
- Tomatillo salsa, shredded Monterey Jack cheese and chopped fresh cilantro

1. Preheat oven to 375°F. Line baking sheet with foil.
2. Combine lime juice, oil, garlic, black pepper and salt in small bowl; mix well. Spread onions and jalapeños on prepared baking sheet; top with pork. Rub pork with oil mixture.
3. Roast pork 45 minutes or until 145°F and barely pink in center. Wrap ends of foil over pork to keep warm; let stand while preparing rolls.
4. Split rolls in half; place cut sides up on another baking sheet. Heat in oven 3 to 5 minutes or until lightly toasted.
5. Thinly slice pork. Serve on rolls with onion and jalapeños; top with salsa, cheese and cilantro. Serve warm.

Comfort Food Casseroles

BAKED PUMPKIN FRENCH TOAST

MAKES 6 SERVINGS

- **1 tablespoon butter, softened**
- **1 loaf challah or egg bread (12 to 16 ounces), cut into ¾-inch-thick slices**
- **7 eggs**
- **1¼ cups whole milk**
- **⅔ cup canned pumpkin**
- **1 teaspoon vanilla**
- **½ teaspoon pumpkin pie spice**
- **⅛ teaspoon salt**
- **3 tablespoons sugar**
- **2 teaspoons ground cinnamon**
- **Maple syrup**

1. Generously grease 13×9-inch baking dish with butter. Arrange bread slices in dish, fitting slices in tightly.
2. Whisk eggs, milk, pumpkin, vanilla, pumpkin pie spice and salt in medium bowl until well blended. Pour over bread; turn slices to coat completely. Cover and refrigerate 8 hours or overnight.
3. Preheat oven to 350°F. Combine sugar and cinnamon in small bowl; mix well. Turn bread slices again; sprinkle generously with cinnamon-sugar.
4. Bake 30 minutes or until bread is puffy and golden brown. Serve immediately with maple syrup.

CHICKEN ENCHILADA BAKE

MAKES 8 SERVINGS

- **1 tablespoon olive oil**
- **1 cup chopped red onion**
- **1 can (4 ounces) diced green chiles**
- **2 cans (10 ounces each) mild enchilada sauce**
- **12 ounces shredded cooked chicken**
- **⅔ cup sliced green onions**
- **12 (6-inch) corn tortillas**
- **1 cup (4 ounces) shredded Mexican cheese blend**
- **Sour cream (optional)**

1. Preheat oven to 350°F. Spray 2½-quart baking dish with nonstick cooking spray.

2. Heat oil in large nonstick skillet over medium-high heat. Add red onion and chiles; cook and stir 4 to 5 minutes or until onion is tender. Stir in enchilada sauce, chicken and green onions.

3. Place four tortillas in bottom of prepared baking dish. Spoon 2 cups chicken mixture over tortillas; top with ⅓ cup cheese. Top with four tortillas, 1 cup chicken mixture and ⅓ cup cheese. Repeat with remaining four tortillas, chicken mixture and cheese.

4. Cover and bake 20 minutes. Uncover; bake 10 minutes or until heated through. Let stand 10 minutes before serving. Serve with sour cream, if desired.

CHEESY SPINACH CASSEROLE

MAKES 6 SERVINGS

- **1 pound baby spinach**
- **4 slices bacon, chopped**
- **1 small onion, chopped**
- **1 cup sliced mushrooms**
- **¼ cup chopped red bell pepper**
- **3 cloves garlic, minced**
- **1½ teaspoons minced canned chipotle peppers in adobo sauce**
- **1 teaspoon seasoned salt**
- **8 ounces pasteurized process cheese product, cut into pieces**
- **½ (8-ounce) package cream cheese, cut into pieces**
- **1 cup thawed frozen corn**
- **½ cup (2 ounces) shredded Monterey Jack and Cheddar cheese blend**

1. Preheat oven to 350°F. Spray 1-quart baking dish with nonstick cooking spray.

2. Bring large saucepan of water to a boil over high heat. Add spinach; cook 1 minute. Drain and transfer to bowl of ice water to stop cooking. Drain and squeeze spinach dry; set aside. Wipe out saucepan with paper towel.

3. Cook bacon in same saucepan over medium-high heat until almost crisp, stirring frequently. Drain off all but 1 tablespoon drippings. Add onion to saucepan; cook and stir 3 minutes or until softened. Add mushrooms and bell pepper; cook and stir 5 minutes or until vegetables are tender. Add garlic, chipotle peppers and seasoned salt; cook and stir 1 minute.

4. Add cheese product and cream cheese to saucepan; cook over medium heat until melted, stirring frequently. Add spinach and corn; cook and stir 3 minutes. Transfer to prepared baking dish; sprinkle with shredded cheese.

5. Bake 20 to 25 minutes or until cheese is melted and casserole is bubbly. If desired, broil 1 to 2 minutes to brown top of casserole.

CAJUN-STYLE BEEF AND BEANS

MAKES 6 SERVINGS

- **1 pound ground beef**
- **¾ cup chopped onion**
- **2½ cups cooked brown rice**
- **1 can (about 15 ounces) kidney beans, rinsed and drained**
- **1 can (about 14 ounces) stewed tomatoes**
- **2 teaspoons Cajun seasoning**
- **¾ cup (3 ounces) shredded Cheddar cheese**

1. Preheat oven to 350°F. Spray 2-quart baking dish with nonstick cooking spray.
2. Cook beef in large skillet over medium-high heat 6 to 8 minutes or until browned, stirring to break up meat. Drain fat.
3. Add onion; cook and stir 2 minutes or until translucent. Stir in rice, beans, tomatoes and Cajun seasoning; mix well. Transfer to prepared baking dish.
4. Cover and bake 25 to 30 minutes, stirring once. Sprinkle with cheese; cover and let stand 5 minutes before serving.

Tip

To make your own Cajun seasoning, combine 5 tablespoons ground red pepper, 3 tablespoons black pepper, 3 tablespoons onion powder, 3 tablespoons garlic powder, 3 tablespoons chili powder, 1 tablespoon dried thyme, 1 tablespoon dried basil and 1 tablespoon ground bay leaf in a medium bowl; mix well. If desired, stir in ½ cup salt. Store in a tightly sealed container.

POTATO AND LEEK GRATIN

MAKES 6 TO 8 SERVINGS

- 5 tablespoons butter, divided
- 2 large leeks, sliced
- 2 tablespoons minced garlic
- 2 pounds baking potatoes, peeled (about 4 medium)
- 1 cup whipping cream
- 1 cup milk
- 3 eggs
- 2 teaspoons salt
- ¼ teaspoon white pepper
- 2 to 3 slices dense day-old white bread, such as French or Italian
- 2 ounces grated Parmesan cheese

1 Preheat oven to 375°F. Generously grease shallow 2½-quart baking dish with 1 tablespoon butter.

2 Melt 2 tablespoons butter in large skillet over medium heat. Add leeks and garlic; cook and stir 8 to 10 minutes or until leeks are softened. Remove from heat.

3 Cut potatoes crosswise into 1/16-inch-thick slices. Layer half of potato slices in prepared baking dish; top with half of leek mixture. Repeat layers. Whisk cream, milk, eggs, salt and pepper in medium bowl until well blended; pour evenly over leek mixture.

4 Tear bread slices into 1-inch pieces. Place in food processor or blender; process until fine crumbs form. Measure ¾ cup crumbs; place in small bowl. Stir in cheese. Melt remaining 2 tablespoons butter; stir into crumb mixture. Sprinkle over vegetables in baking dish.

5 Bake 1 hour 15 minutes or until top is golden brown and potatoes are tender. Let stand 5 to 10 minutes before serving.

COUNTRY CHICKEN POT PIE

MAKES 6 SERVINGS

- 2 tablespoons butter
- 1 pound boneless skinless chicken breasts, cut into 1-inch pieces
- ¾ teaspoon salt
- 8 ounces fresh green beans, cut into 1-inch pieces (2 cups)
- ½ cup chopped red bell pepper
- ½ cup thinly sliced celery
- 3 tablespoons all-purpose flour
- ½ cup chicken broth
- ½ cup half-and-half
- 1 teaspoon dried thyme
- ½ teaspoon dried sage
- 1 cup frozen pearl onions
- ½ cup frozen corn
- Pie crust for single-crust 10-inch pie

1. Preheat oven to 425°F. Spray 10-inch deep-dish pie plate with nonstick cooking spray.
2. Melt butter in large skillet over medium-high heat. Add chicken; cook and stir 3 minutes or until no longer pink in center. Sprinkle with salt. Add beans, bell pepper and celery; cook and stir 3 minutes.
3. Sprinkle flour over chicken and vegetables; cook and stir 1 minute. Stir in broth, half-and-half, thyme and sage; bring to a boil over high heat. Reduce heat to low; cook 3 minutes or until sauce is thickened. Stir in onions and corn. Return to a simmer; cook and stir 1 minute.
4. Transfer mixture to prepared pie plate. Place pie crust over filling; turn edge under and flute or crimp. Cut four slits in top of crust with tip of knife.
5. Bake 20 minutes or until filling is hot and bubbly and crust is golden brown. Let stand 5 minutes before serving.

HAM AND CHEESE BREAD PUDDING

MAKES 8 SERVINGS

- **1 small loaf (8 ounces) sourdough, country French or Italian bread, sliced**
- **3 tablespoons butter, softened**
- **8 ounces ham or smoked ham, cubed**
- **1 cup (4 ounces) shredded Cheddar cheese**
- **3 eggs**
- **2 cups milk**
- **1 teaspoon ground mustard**
- **½ teaspoon salt**
- **⅛ teaspoon white pepper**

1 Spray 11×7-inch baking dish with nonstick cooking spray. Spread one side of each bread slice with butter. Cut bread into 1-inch cubes; place in prepared baking dish. Top with ham; sprinkle with cheese.

2 Beat eggs in medium bowl. Whisk in milk, mustard, salt and pepper until blended. Pour egg mixture evenly over bread mixture; cover and refrigerate at least 6 hours or overnight.

3 Preheat oven to 350°F. Bake, uncovered, 45 to 50 minutes or until puffed and golden brown and knife inserted into center comes out clean. Serve immediately.

FIESTA BEEF ENCHILADAS

MAKES 2 SERVINGS

- 6 ounces ground beef
- ¼ cup sliced green onions
- 1 teaspoon minced garlic
- ½ cup mild or hot red or green enchilada sauce
- 1 cup (4 ounces) shredded Mexican cheese blend or Cheddar cheese, divided
- ¾ cup chopped tomato, divided
- ½ cup frozen corn, thawed
- ½ cup cooked black beans
- ⅓ cup cooked white or brown rice
- ¼ cup salsa or picante sauce
- 6 (6-inch) corn tortillas
- 2 sheets (20×12 inches each) heavy-duty foil, generously sprayed with nonstick cooking spray
- ½ cup sliced romaine lettuce

1. Preheat oven to 375°F. Cook beef in large skillet over medium-high heat 6 to 8 minutes or until browned, stirring to break up meat. Drain fat. Add green onions and garlic; cook and stir 2 minutes.

2. Combine beef mixture, enchilada sauce, ¾ cup cheese, ½ cup tomato, corn, beans, rice and salsa in large bowl; mix well. Spoon mixture down center of tortillas; roll up to enclose filling. Place three enchiladas, seam side down, on each foil sheet.

3. Double fold sides and ends of foil to seal packets, leaving head space for heat circulation. Place packets on large baking sheet.

4. Bake 15 minutes. Remove from oven; open packets and sprinkle with remaining ¼ cup cheese. Reseal packets; bake 10 minutes or until cheese is melted. Serve with lettuce and remaining ¼ cup tomato.

SCALLOPED SWEET POTATOES

MAKES 8 SERVINGS

- **4 medium sweet potatoes (2 pounds)**
- **4 slices bacon**
- **1 small onion, chopped**
- **2½ tablespoons all-purpose flour**
- **2 cups milk**
- **½ teaspoon salt**
- **¼ teaspoon black pepper**
- **1¼ cups grated Parmesan cheese**

1. Preheat oven to 325°F. Peel potatoes; cut into ¼-inch slices. Bring large saucepan of water to a boil. Add sweet potatoes; cook 5 to 10 minutes or until almost tender. Drain well; set aside.

2. Meanwhile, cook bacon in large skillet over medium-high heat until crisp. Drain on paper towel-lined plate; crumble into small pieces.

3. Add onion to bacon drippings in skillet; cook 5 minutes or until tender, stirring occasionally. Reduce heat to low; stir in flour and cook to a paste. Add milk, salt and pepper; cook and stir over medium heat until mixture thickens slightly.

4. Spread half of sweet potatoes in 11×7-inch baking dish; sprinkle with half of bacon. Pour half of milk mixture over sweet potatoes; repeat layers. Sprinkle with cheese.

5. Bake 20 minutes or until sweet potatoes are tender. If desired, broil casserole 1 to 2 minutes until cheese is lightly browned.

HEARTY TACO CASSEROLE

MAKES 8 SERVINGS

- **1 pound ground beef**
- **1 pound ground pork***
- **1 onion, chopped**
- **1 green bell pepper, chopped**
- **2 cloves garlic, minced**
- **2 packages (about 1 ounce each) taco seasoning mix**
- **1 cup water**
- **1 package (16 ounces) frozen corn**
- **1 jar (24 ounces) chunky salsa**
- **3 cups (12 ounces) shredded Mexican cheese blend**
- **Tortilla chips or flour tortillas**

Or use 2 pounds ground beef instead of 1 pound each ground beef and pork.

1 Preheat oven to 350°F. Spray 13×9-inch baking dish with nonstick cooking spray.

2 Cook beef and pork in large skillet over medium-high heat about 5 minutes or until meat is no longer pink, stirring to break up meat. Drain fat.

3 Add onion, bell pepper and garlic; cook and stir about 5 minutes or until meat is browned and vegetables are softened. Stir in taco seasoning and water until well blended. Stir in corn; bring to a simmer. Reduce heat to medium-low; cook 10 minutes, stirring occasionally.

4 Spread half of meat mixture in prepared baking dish. Spread half of salsa over meat mixture; sprinkle with 2 cups cheese. Top with remaining meat mixture and salsa.

5 Bake 30 to 35 minutes or until casserole is bubbly and heated through. Sprinkle with remaining 1 cup cheese; bake 2 to 3 minutes or until cheese is melted. Serve with tortilla chips.

BISCUIT-TOPPED STEAK AND VEGETABLE PIE

MAKES 6 SERVINGS

- **1½ pounds boneless top round steak, cooked and cut into 1-inch pieces**
- **1 package (9 ounces) frozen baby carrots**
- **1 package (9 ounces) frozen peas and pearl onions**
- **1 large baking potato, baked, peeled and cut into ½-inch pieces**
- **1 jar (18 ounces) homestyle brown gravy**
- **½ teaspoon dried thyme**
- **½ teaspoon black pepper**
- **1 container (10 ounces) refrigerated flaky buttermilk biscuits**

1. Preheat oven to 375°F. Spray 2-quart baking dish with nonstick cooking spray.

2. Combine steak, carrots, peas and onions, potato, gravy, thyme and pepper in large bowl; mix well. Pour into prepared baking dish.

3. Bake 40 minutes. Remove from oven; *increase oven temperature to 400°F.* Top with biscuits; bake 8 to 10 minutes or until biscuits are golden brown.

Variations

This casserole can be prepared with leftovers of almost any kind. Other types of steak, roast beef, stew meat, pork or chicken can be substituted for the round steak; adjust the gravy flavor to complement the meat. Red potatoes can be used instead of the baking potato, and other vegetable combinations, such as broccoli, cauliflower and carrots or broccoli, corn and red peppers, can be used instead of the carrots, peas and onions.

CHILES RELLENOS CASSEROLE

MAKES 4 SERVINGS

- **3 eggs, separated**
- **¾ cup milk**
- **¾ cup all-purpose flour**
- **½ teaspoon salt**
- **1 tablespoon butter**
- **½ cup chopped onion**
- **2 cans (7 ounces each) whole green chiles, drained**
- **8 slices (1 ounce each) Monterey Jack cheese, cut into halves**
- **Optional toppings: sliced green onions, sliced olives, guacamole and salsa**

1. Preheat oven to 350°F. Spray 13×9-inch baking dish with nonstick cooking spray.
2. Combine egg yolks, milk, flour and salt in food processor or blender; process until smooth. Pour into large bowl.
3. Melt butter in small skillet over medium heat. Add onion; cook and stir 3 minutes or until tender.
4. Pat chiles dry with paper towels. Slit each chile lengthwise; remove seeds. Place two halves of cheese slice and 1 tablespoon onion in each chile; reshape chiles to cover cheese. Place filled chiles in single layer in prepared baking dish.
5. Beat egg whites in medium bowl with electric mixer at medium-high speed until soft peaks form; fold into egg yolk mixture. Pour over chiles in baking dish.
6. Bake 20 to 25 minutes or until casserole is puffed and knife inserted into center comes out clean. *Turn oven to broil;* broil 4 inches from heat source 30 seconds or until top is golden brown. Serve with desired toppings.

SOUTHWEST TURKEY BAKE

MAKES 8 SERVINGS

- 1 tablespoon vegetable oil
- 1 pound ground turkey
- 1 can (about 15 ounces) black beans, rinsed and drained
- 1 cup salsa
- ½ teaspoon salt
- ½ teaspoon ground cumin
- ⅛ teaspoon ground red pepper
- 1 package (8½ ounces) corn muffin mix
- ¾ cup chicken broth
- 1 egg
- ¾ cup (3 ounces) shredded Mexican cheese blend
- Lime wedges (optional)

1. Preheat oven to 400°F. Spray 13×9-inch baking dish with nonstick cooking spray.
2. Heat oil in large skillet over medium-high heat. Add turkey; cook 6 to 8 minutes or until no longer pink, stirring to break up meat.
3. Add beans, salsa, salt, cumin and red pepper; cook and stir 2 minutes. Transfer to prepared baking dish.
4. Combine corn muffin mix, broth and egg in medium bowl; mix well. Spread batter over turkey mixture; sprinkle with cheese.
5. Bake 15 minutes or until edges of topping are lightly browned. Serve with lime wedges, if desired.

SPINACH ARTICHOKE GRATIN

MAKES 6 SERVINGS

- **2 cups (16 ounces) cottage cheese**
- **2 eggs**
- **6 tablespoons grated Parmesan cheese, divided**
- **1 tablespoon lemon juice**
- **½ teaspoon salt**
- **⅛ teaspoon black pepper**
- **⅛ teaspoon ground nutmeg**
- **2 packages (10 ounces each) frozen chopped spinach, thawed**
- **⅓ cup thinly sliced green onions**
- **1 package (10 ounces) frozen artichoke hearts, thawed and halved**

1. Preheat oven to 375°F. Spray 1½-quart baking dish with nonstick cooking spray.
2. Combine cottage cheese, eggs, ¼ cup Parmesan, lemon juice, salt, pepper and nutmeg in food processor or blender; process until smooth.
3. Squeeze moisture from spinach. Combine spinach, cottage cheese mixture and green onions in large bowl; mix well. Spread half of mixture in prepared baking dish.
4. Pat artichokes dry with paper towels; spread evenly over spinach mixture. Sprinkle with remaining 2 tablespoons Parmesan; top with remaining spinach mixture.
5. Cover and bake 25 minutes.

MEXICAN LASAGNA

MAKES 4 SERVINGS

- **1 pound ground beef**
- **1 package (about 1 ounce) taco seasoning mix**
- **1 can (about 14 ounces) Mexican-style diced tomatoes**
- **1½ teaspoons chili powder**
- **1 teaspoon ground cumin**
- **½ teaspoon salt**
- **½ teaspoon red pepper flakes**
- **2 cups sour cream**
- **6 green onions, chopped**
- **1 can (4 ounces) diced green chiles**
- **6 to 7 (8-inch) flour tortillas**
- **1 can (15 ounces) corn, drained**
- **2 cups (8 ounces) shredded Cheddar cheese**

1. Preheat oven to 350°F. Spray 13×9-inch baking dish with nonstick cooking spray.
2. Cook beef and taco seasoning in large skillet over medium heat 6 to 8 minutes or until browned, stirring to break up meat. Drain fat.
3. Combine tomatoes, chili powder, cumin, salt and red pepper flakes in medium bowl; mix well. Combine sour cream, green onions and chiles in small bowl.
4. Spread one third of tomato mixture in prepared baking dish. Top with two tortillas, one third of sour cream mixture, one third of beef mixture, one third of corn and one third of cheese. Repeat layers twice.
5. Bake 35 minutes or until bubbly. Let stand 15 minutes before serving.

Super Satisfying Sweet Things

CHOCOLATE CHUNK PIZZA COOKIE

MAKES 3 PIZZA COOKIES (2 TO 3 SERVINGS EACH)

- 2 cups all-purpose flour
- 1 teaspoon baking soda
- 1 teaspoon salt
- ¾ cup (1½ sticks) butter, softened
- 1 cup packed brown sugar
- ¼ cup granulated sugar
- 2 eggs
- 1 teaspoon vanilla
- 1 package (about 11 ounces) chocolate chunks
- Vanilla ice cream

1. Preheat oven to 400°F. Spray three 6-inch cast iron skillets, cake pans or deep-dish pizza pans with nonstick cooking spray.*

2. Combine flour, baking soda and salt in medium bowl; mix well. Beat butter, brown sugar and granulated sugar in large bowl with electric mixer at medium speed about 3 minutes or until creamy. Beat in eggs and vanilla until well blended. Gradually beat in flour mixture at low speed just until blended. Stir in chocolate chunks. Spread dough evenly in prepared skillets.

3. Bake about 15 minutes or until top and edges are deep golden brown but center is still slightly soft. Top with ice cream. Serve warm.

**If you don't have three skillets or pans, you can bake one cookie at a time. Refrigerate dough between batches and make sure skillet is completely cool before adding more dough. (Clean and spray skillet again before adding each new batch.)*

BLACK FOREST COBBLER

MAKES 8 TO 10 SERVINGS

Filling

- 3 pounds frozen pitted sweet cherries, thawed and drained
- ¾ cup sugar
- ¼ cup cornstarch
- 2 tablespoons lemon juice
- 1 teaspoon vanilla

Biscuit Topping

- 1¼ cups all-purpose flour
- ½ cup sugar
- ¼ cup unsweetened cocoa powder
- 1½ teaspoons baking powder
- 1 teaspoon baking soda
- ½ teaspoon salt
- 6 tablespoons (¾ stick) cold butter, cut into small pieces
- ½ cup semisweet chocolate chips
- ⅔ cup buttermilk

1. Preheat oven to 375°F. Spray 9-inch square baking dish with nonstick cooking spray.

2. For filling, combine cherries, ¾ cup sugar, cornstarch, lemon juice and vanilla in large bowl; toss to coat. Spoon into prepared baking dish.

3. For topping, combine flour, ½ cup sugar, cocoa, baking powder, baking soda and salt in medium bowl; mix well. Cut in butter with pastry blender or mix with fingertips until mixture resembles coarse crumbs. Stir in chocolate chips. Add buttermilk; stir just until combined. (Do not overmix.) Drop topping, 2 tablespoonfuls at a time, into mounds over cherry mixture.

4. Bake 40 to 45 minutes or until filling is bubbly and toothpick inserted into center of topping comes out clean. Let stand 30 minutes before serving. Serve warm.

STRAWBERRY MOUSSE

MAKES 4 TO 6 SERVINGS

- **1 package (4-serving size) strawberry gelatin**
- **½ cup boiling water**
- **2 cups sliced fresh strawberries, divided**
- **½ cup cream cheese, softened**
- **½ cup cold water**
- **¼ teaspoon almond extract**
- **1 cup whipped topping, plus additional for garnish**

1. Place gelatin in small bowl. Pour boiling water over gelatin; stir until completely dissolved.
2. Pour gelatin mixture into blender. Add 1 cup strawberries, cream cheese, cold water and almond extract; blend 1 minute or until completely smooth. Pour mixture into medium bowl. Add 1 cup whipped topping; whisk until well blended (make sure gelatin mix does not settle to bottom of bowl).
3. Spoon mousse into dessert glasses or dishes; refrigerate at least 2 hours or until set. Top with remaining 1 cup strawberries and additional whipped topping, if desired.

WARM CHOCOLATE CAKES

MAKES 4 CAKES

- ½ cup (1 stick) butter, plus additional for greasing cups
- 4 ounces bittersweet or semisweet chocolate, chopped
- 2 eggs
- 2 egg yolks
- ¼ cup granulated sugar
- ¼ cup all-purpose flour
- ¼ teaspoon salt
- Powdered sugar (optional)

1. Preheat oven to 400°F. Butter four ¾-cup custard cups or soufflé dishes; place on baking sheet.
2. Melt ½ cup butter and chocolate in microwave or in small saucepan over very low heat; set aside to cool slightly.
3. Meanwhile, beat eggs, egg yolks and granulated sugar in medium bowl with electric mixer at medium speed about 5 minutes or until thick and light in color.
4. Add flour and salt; beat just until blended. Gently fold in chocolate mixture. Pour into prepared custard cups.
5. Bake about 9 minutes or until edges of cakes are set but centers are soft and move slightly when shaken. Let stand 2 minutes; invert cakes onto serving plates. Sprinkle with powdered sugar, if desired.

Tip

The cakes can be made several hours in advance and baked just before serving. Prepare batter as directed; cover and refrigerate until ready to bake. Bake at 400°F 10 to 11 minutes.

CRUNCHY ICE CREAM PIE >

MAKES 6 SERVINGS

- 8 ounces semisweet chocolate, chopped
- 2 tablespoons butter
- 1½ cups crisp rice cereal
- ½ gallon chocolate chip or fudge ripple ice cream, softened
- Hot fudge topping

1. Spray 9-inch pie plate with nonstick cooking spray.
2. Melt chocolate and butter in medium saucepan over very low heat. Remove from heat; stir in cereal until well blended.
3. Spoon mixture into prepared pie plate; press onto bottom and 1 inch up side to form crust. Spread ice cream evenly in crust. Cover and freeze until ready to serve.
4. Let pie stand at room temperature 10 minutes before serving. Drizzle with hot fudge topping.

SUPER FUDGY BROWNIES

MAKES 16 BROWNIES

- ½ cup all-purpose flour
- ½ cup unsweetened cocoa powder
- ½ teaspoon salt
- ½ cup (1 stick) butter
- 1 cup sugar
- 2 eggs
- 1 teaspoon vanilla
- ¾ cup semisweet or bittersweet chocolate chips

1. Preheat oven to 350°F. Spray 8-inch square baking pan with nonstick cooking spray. Line with parchment paper, leaving overhang on two sides, and spray again.
2. Sift flour, cocoa and salt into small bowl. Melt butter in medium saucepan over medium heat. Remove from heat; add sugar and whisk 2 minutes. Add eggs and vanilla; whisk 1 minute or until very well blended. Add flour mixture; stir just until blended. Stir in chocolate chips. Spread batter in prepared pan; smooth top.
3. Bake 20 to 22 minutes or until edges are set and toothpick inserted into center comes out with moist crumbs. Cool completely in pan on wire rack. Remove from pan using parchment; cut into bars.

SOUTHERN CARAMEL APPLE BARS

MAKES ABOUT 2 TO 3 DOZEN BARS

- 2 cups all-purpose flour
- 1 teaspoon salt
- ½ teaspoon baking powder
- ½ teaspoon baking soda
- ⅔ cup butter
- ¾ cup packed brown sugar
- ½ cup granulated sugar
- 1 egg
- 1 teaspoon vanilla
- 4 Granny Smith apples, peeled and coarsely chopped
- ½ cup pecans, chopped
- 24 caramel candies, unwrapped
- 2 tablespoons milk

1. Preheat oven to 350°F. Spray 13×9-inch baking pan with nonstick cooking spray.

2. Combine flour, salt, baking powder and baking soda in medium bowl; mix well. Melt butter in large saucepan over medium heat. Remove from heat; stir in brown sugar and granulated sugar. Add egg and vanilla; stir until well blended. Add flour mixture; stir until blended. Press into bottom of prepared pan; top with apples.

3. Bake 40 to 45 minutes or until edges are browned and pulling away from sides of pan. Cool completely in pan on wire rack.

4. Toast pecans in medium nonstick skillet over medium-high heat 2 minutes or until fragrant, stirring frequently. Remove to small bowl; set aside. Wipe out skillet with paper towel. Add caramels and milk to skillet; cook over medium-low heat until melted and smooth, stirring constantly.

5. Drizzle caramel sauce over cooled apple bars; sprinkle with pecans. Let stand 30 minutes before cutting into bars.

CHOCOLATE PEANUT BUTTER PUDDING CAKE

MAKES ABOUT 8 SERVINGS

- 1¼ cups granulated sugar, divided
- 1 cup all-purpose flour
- ½ cup unsweetened cocoa powder, divided
- 1 teaspoon baking powder
- 1 teaspoon baking soda
- ¼ teaspoon salt
- ½ cup sour cream
- ½ cup creamy peanut butter
- 3 tablespoons butter, melted
- 4 tablespoons hot water
- ¼ cup packed brown sugar
- 1½ cups boiling water
- Whipped cream (optional)

1. Preheat oven to 350°F. Spray 8-inch square baking dish with nonstick cooking spray.
2. Combine ¾ cup granulated sugar, flour, ¼ cup cocoa, baking powder, baking soda and salt in large bowl; mix well.
3. Whisk sour cream, peanut butter and melted butter in medium bowl until well blended. Gradually whisk in 4 tablespoons hot water until smooth. Add to flour mixture, stir until well blended. (Batter will be thick.) Spread batter in prepared baking dish; smooth top.
4. Combine remaining ½ cup granulated sugar, ¼ cup cocoa and brown sugar in small bowl; mix well. Sprinkle evenly over batter. Pour boiling water over sugar layer (do not stir).
5. Bake about 35 minutes or until center is almost set. Let stand 10 minutes before serving. Serve cake in bowls or dessert dishes, spooning sauce from bottom of dish over cake. Top with whipped cream, if desired.

BROWN BUTTER BLUEBERRY PEACH COBBLER

MAKES 8 SERVINGS

- **3 tablespoons butter**
- **4 packages (16 ounces each) frozen sliced peaches, thawed and drained**
- **1 cup fresh blueberries**
- **½ cup packed brown sugar**
- **¼ cup all-purpose flour**
- **½ teaspoon vanilla**
- **¼ teaspoon ground nutmeg**
- **1¼ cups biscuit baking mix**
- **⅓ cup milk**
- **2 tablespoons butter, melted**
- **2 tablespoons granulated sugar**

1. Preheat oven to 375°F.
2. Melt 3 tablespoons butter in large skillet (not nonstick) over medium heat. Cook and stir 3 minutes or until butter has nutty aroma and turns light brown in color. Add peaches; cook and stir 2 minutes.
3. Combine peaches, blueberries, brown sugar, flour, vanilla and nutmeg in large bowl; toss gently to coat. Spoon into 2-quart baking dish.
4. Bake 10 minutes. Meanwhile, combine baking mix, milk, 2 tablespoons melted butter and granulated sugar in medium bowl; mix well. Drop batter in eight equal spoonfuls over warm fruit mixture.
5. Bake 30 to 35 minutes or until topping is deep golden brown and cooked on bottom. Cool 10 minutes. Serve warm.

BANANA CREAM PIE

MAKES 8 SERVINGS

- **1 refrigerated pie crust (half of 14-ounce package)**
- **⅔ cup sugar**
- **¼ cup cornstarch**
- **¼ teaspoon salt**
- **2½ cups milk**
- **4 egg yolks, beaten**
- **2 tablespoons butter, softened**
- **2 teaspoons vanilla**
- **2 medium bananas**
- **1 teaspoon lemon juice**
- **Whipped cream and toasted sliced almonds (optional)**

1. Preheat oven to 400°F. Line 9-inch pie plate with crust; flute edge. Prick bottom and side all over with fork. Bake 10 minutes or until crust is golden brown. Cool completely on wire rack.

2. Combine sugar, cornstarch and salt in medium saucepan; whisk in milk until well blended. Cook over medium heat about 12 minutes or until mixture boils and thickens, whisking constantly. Boil 2 minutes, whisking constantly. Remove from heat.

3. Gradually whisk ½ cup hot milk mixture into egg yolks in small bowl. Gradually whisk mixture back into milk mixture in saucepan. Cook over medium heat about 5 minutes, whisking constantly. Remove from heat; whisk in butter and vanilla. Cool 20 minutes, stirring occasionally. Strain through fine-mesh strainer into medium bowl. Press plastic wrap onto surface of pudding; cool about 30 minutes or until lukewarm.

4. Cut bananas into ¼-inch slices; toss with lemon juice in medium bowl. Spread half of pudding in cooled crust; arrange bananas over pudding. (Reserve several slices for garnish, if desired.) Spread remaining pudding over bananas; refrigerate 4 hours or overnight. Garnish with whipped cream, almonds and reserved banana slices.

DOUBLE CHOCOLATE COOKIES AND CREAM MOUSSE

MAKES 8 SERVINGS

- **8 ounces semisweet chocolate, chopped**
- **2½ cups chilled whipping cream, divided**
- **4 egg yolks**
- **Pinch salt**
- **1¼ teaspoons vanilla, divided**
- **¼ cup granulated sugar**
- **23 chocolate sandwich cookies, divided**
- **1 tablespoon powdered sugar**

1. Melt chocolate in medium saucepan over very low heat, stirring frequently. Remove from heat; stir in ¼ cup cream until well blended.
2. Combine egg yolks and pinch of salt in medium bowl. Whisk about half of chocolate mixture into egg yolks until blended; whisk egg yolk mixture back into chocolate mixture in saucepan. Cook over low heat 2 minutes, whisking constantly. Remove from heat; cool to room temperature.
3. Beat 1¾ cups cream and 1 teaspoon vanilla in large bowl with electric mixer at high speed until soft peaks form. Gradually beat in granulated sugar; beat until stiff peaks form. Fold about one fourth of whipped cream into chocolate mixture; fold chocolate mixture into remaining whipped cream until completely combined.
4. Finely chop 2 cookies; fold into mousse. Coarsely chop 2 cookies for topping. Cut remaining 19 cookies into quarters; set aside. Refrigerate mousse 4 hours or overnight.
5. Beat remaining ½ cup cream in medium bowl with electric mixer at high speed 30 seconds or until thickened. Add powdered sugar and remaining ¼ teaspoon vanilla; beat until stiff peaks form.
6. Spoon ¼ cup mousse into each of eight wide-mouth half-pint jars or serving bowls. Top with ¼ cup quartered cookies and another ¼ cup mousse. Garnish with dollop of sweetened whipped cream and chopped cookies.

CLASSIC PEANUT BUTTER COOKIES

MAKES 3 DOZEN COOKIES

- **1¼ cups all-purpose flour**
- **½ teaspoon baking powder**
- **½ teaspoon baking soda**
- **½ teaspoon salt**
- **⅔ cup creamy peanut buter**
- **½ cup (1 stick) butter, softened**
- **½ cup granulated sugar**
- **½ cup packed dark brown sugar**
- **1 egg**

1. Combine flour, baking powder, baking soda and salt in small bowl; mix well.
2. Beat peanut butter, butter, granulated sugar and brown sugar in large bowl with electric mixer at medium speed 2 minutes or until smooth and creamy. Add egg; beat 1 minute or until well blended. Add flour mixture; beat at low speed just until blended. Refrigerate dough 20 minutes for easier handling.
3. Preheat oven to 350°F. Shape tablespoonfuls of dough into balls; place 2 inches apart on ungreased cookie sheets. Gently flatten cookies with fork, pressing crisscross pattern into top of dough.
4. Bake 12 to 14 minutes or until edges begin to brown. Remove to wire racks to cool completely.

WARM APPLE CROSTATA

MAKES 4 TARTS (4 TO 8 SERVINGS)

- 1¾ cups all-purpose flour
- ⅓ cup granulated sugar
- ½ teaspoon plus ⅛ teaspoon salt, divided
- ¾ cup (1½ sticks) cold butter, cut into small pieces
- 3 tablespoons ice water
- 2 teaspoons vanilla
- 8 Pink Lady or Honeycrisp apples (about 1½ pounds), peeled and cut into ¼-inch slices
- ¼ cup packed brown sugar
- 1 tablespoon lemon juice
- 1 teaspoon ground cinnamon
- ⅛ teaspoon ground nutmeg
- 4 teaspoons butter, cut into very small pieces
- 1 egg, beaten
- 1 to 2 teaspoons coarse sugar
- Vanilla ice cream
- Caramel sauce or ice cream topping

1. Combine flour, granulated sugar and ½ teaspoon salt in food processor; process 5 seconds. Add ¾ cup cold butter; process 10 seconds or until mixture resembles coarse crumbs.

2. Combine ice water and vanilla in small bowl. With motor running, pour mixture through feed tube; process 12 seconds or until dough begins to come together. Shape dough into a disc; wrap with plastic wrap and refrigerate 30 minutes.

3. Meanwhile, combine apples, brown sugar, lemon juice, cinnamon, nutmeg and remaining ⅛ teaspoon salt in large bowl; toss to coat. Preheat oven to 400°F.

4. Line two baking sheets with parchment paper. Cut dough into four pieces; roll out each piece into 7-inch circle on floured surface. Place on prepared baking sheets; mound apples in center of dough circles (about 1 cup apples for each crostata). Fold or roll up edges of dough towards center to create rim of crostata.

5. Dot apples with 4 teaspoons butter. Brush dough with egg; sprinkle dough and apples with coarse sugar.

6. Bake 20 minutes or until apples are tender and crust is golden brown. Serve warm topped with ice cream and caramel sauce.

ST. LOUIS GOOEY BUTTER CAKE

MAKES 12 TO 15 SERVINGS

- **1 package (about 15 ounces) yellow cake mix**
- **½ cup (1 stick) butter, melted**
- **4 eggs, divided**
- **1 package (8 ounces) cream cheese, softened**
- **1 teaspoon vanilla**
- **3 cups powdered sugar, plus additional for garnish**

1. Preheat oven to 350°F. Spray 13×9-inch baking pan with nonstick cooking spray.
2. Beat cake mix, butter and 2 eggs in large bowl with electric mixer at low speed 1 minute or just until blended. Press mixture evenly into bottom of prepared pan.
3. Beat cream cheese, remaining 2 eggs and vanilla in medium bowl with electric mixer at medium-high speed 1 minute or until well blended. Slowly add 3 cups powdered sugar; beat until smooth. Spread batter evenly over cake mix layer in pan.
4. Bake 35 to 40 minutes or until top is lightly browned. (Cake will puff up and then collapse during baking to make gooey center.) Cool completely in pan on wire rack. Sprinkle with additional powdered sugar, if desired.

FRENCH SILK PIE

MAKES 8 SERVINGS

- **1 (9-inch) deep-dish pie crust (frozen or refrigerated)**
- **1⅓ cups granulated sugar**
- **¾ cup (1½ sticks) butter, softened**
- **4 ounces unsweetened chocolate, melted**
- **1½ tablespoons unsweetened cocoa powder**
- **1 teaspoon vanilla**
- **⅛ teaspoon salt**
- **4 pasteurized eggs***
- **1 cup whipping cream**
- **2 tablespoons powdered sugar**
- **Chocolate curls (optional)**

****The eggs in this recipe are not cooked, so use pasteurized eggs to ensure food safety.***

1. Bake pie crust according to package directions. Cool completely on wire rack.
2. Beat granulated sugar and butter in large bowl with electric mixer at medium speed 4 minutes or until light and fluffy. Add melted chocolate, cocoa, vanilla and salt; beat until well blended. Add eggs, one at a time, beating 4 minutes after each addition and scraping down side of bowl occasionally.
3. Spread filling in cooled crust. Refrigerate at least 3 hours or overnight.
4. Beat cream and powdered sugar in medium bowl with electric mixer at high speed until soft peaks form. Pipe or spread whipped cream over chocolate layer; garnish with chocolate curls.

APPLE CRANBERRY CRISP

MAKES 6 TO 8 SERVINGS

- **1 cup packed brown sugar, divided**
- **1 tablespoon cornstarch**
- **1 teaspoon ground cinnamon**
- **½ teaspoon ground ginger**
- **¼ teaspoon ground nutmeg**
- **5 to 6 cups cubed peeled tart apples**
- **1 cup fresh or frozen cranberries *or* ½ cup dried cranberries**
- **1 teaspoon grated orange peel**
- **½ cup buttermilk baking mix**
- **½ cup old-fashioned oats**
- **½ cup coarsely chopped walnuts**
- **¼ teaspoon salt**
- **¼ cup (½ stick) cold butter, cut into small pieces**
- **Vanilla ice cream (optional)**

1. Preheat oven to 350°F. Spray 2-quart baking dish with nonstick cooking spray.

2. Combine ½ cup brown sugar, cornstarch, cinnamon, ginger and nutmeg in large bowl; mix well. Add apples, cranberries and orange peel; toss to coat. Spoon into prepared baking dish.

3. Combine baking mix, oats, nuts, remaining ½ cup brown sugar and salt in medium bowl; mix well. Cut in butter with pastry blender until mixture resembles coarse crumbs. Sprinkle over fruit mixture.

4. Bake 50 minutes or until apples are tender. Serve warm with ice cream, if desired.

Index

Index

Index

Metric Conversion Chart

VOLUME MEASUREMENTS (dry)

1/8 teaspoon = 0.5 mL
1/4 teaspoon = 1 mL
1/2 teaspoon = 2 mL
3/4 teaspoon = 4 mL
1 teaspoon = 5 mL
1 tablespoon = 15 mL
2 tablespoons = 30 mL
1/4 cup = 60 mL
1/3 cup = 75 mL
1/2 cup = 125 mL
2/3 cup = 150 mL
3/4 cup = 175 mL
1 cup = 250 mL
2 cups = 1 pint = 500 mL
3 cups = 750 mL
4 cups = 1 quart = 1 L

VOLUME MEASUREMENTS (fluid)

1 fluid ounce (2 tablespoons) = 30 mL
4 fluid ounces (1/2 cup) = 125 mL
8 fluid ounces (1 cup) = 250 mL
12 fluid ounces (1 1/2 cups) = 375 mL
16 fluid ounces (2 cups) = 500 mL

WEIGHTS (mass)

1/2 ounce = 15 g
1 ounce = 30 g
3 ounces = 90 g
4 ounces = 120 g
8 ounces = 225 g
10 ounces = 285 g
12 ounces = 360 g
16 ounces = 1 pound = 450 g

DIMENSIONS

1/16 inch = 2 mm
1/8 inch = 3 mm
1/4 inch = 6 mm
1/2 inch = 1.5 cm
3/4 inch = 2 cm
1 inch = 2.5 cm

OVEN TEMPERATURES

250°F = 120°C
275°F = 140°C
300°F = 150°C
325°F = 160°C
350°F = 180°C
375°F = 190°C
400°F = 200°C
425°F = 220°C
450°F = 230°C

BAKING PAN SIZES

Utensil	Size in Inches/Quarts	Metric Volume	Size in Centimeters
Baking or Cake Pan (square or rectangular)	8×8×2	2 L	20×20×5
	9×9×2	2.5 L	23×23×5
	12×8×2	3 L	30×20×5
	13×9×2	3.5 L	33×23×5
Loaf Pan	8×4×3	1.5 L	20×10×7
	9×5×3	2 L	23×13×7
Round Layer Cake Pan	8×1½	1.2 L	20×4
	9×1½	1.5 L	23×4
Pie Plate	8×1¼	750 mL	20×3
	9×1¼	1 L	23×3
Baking Dish or Casserole	1 quart	1 L	—
	1½ quart	1.5 L	—
	2 quart	2 L	—